STORIES FROM
RESPONSE-CENTERED CLASSROOMS:

Speaking, Questioning, and Theorizing from the Center of the Action

STORIES FROM RESPONSE-CENTERED CLASSROOMS:
Speaking, Questioning, and Theorizing from the Center of the Action

Barbara Smith Livdahl
Karla Smart
Joyce Wallman
Teresa Krinke Herbert
Debra Kramer Geiger
Janice L. Anderson

FOREWORD by Vito Perrone

Teachers College, Columbia University
New York and London

Published by Teachers College Press, 1234 Amsterdam Avenue, New York, NY 10027

Library of Congress Cataloging-in-Publication Data

Stories from response-centered classrooms: speaking, questioning, and
    theorizing from the center of the action / Barbara Smith Livdahl . . .
    [et al.] ; foreword by Vito Perrone.
        p.   cm.
    Includes bibliographical references (p.   ) and index.
    ISBN 0-8077-3458-6.—ISBN 0-8077-3457-8 (pbk.)
        1. Interaction analysis in education.   2. Interpersonal relations.
    3. Language arts—Study and teaching.   I. Livdahl, Barbara Smith.
    LB1034.S86   1995
    371.1′022—dc20   95-9225

    ISBN 0-8077-3457-8 (paper)
    ISBN 0-8077-3458-6 (cloth)
    Printed on acid-free paper
    Manufactured in the United States of America
    01 00 99 98 97 96 95   8 7 6 5 4 3 2 1

to the teachers
who know
or don't know
but give us the power to find knowledge ourselves

who hear
or don't hear
but give us the responsibility of listening

who see
or don't see
but give us the vision to view our world

who touch
or don't touch
but give us the grace to reach out to others

who are truth tellers
or not
but authorize us to find our truths within ourselves

we thank you.
—Janice L. Anderson

Contents

Foreword

At an earlier time in our history, in particular in the latter part of the nineteenth century and the early years of the twentieth century, those who wrote most authoritatively about teaching and learning practice in schools were classroom teachers. Out of these accounts grew the understanding that theory and practice were reciprocal, fully integrated formulations. In the middle to later years of the twentieth century, however, writing about classroom practice has tended to move away from the schools and into the colleges and universities. In the process, it has become less interesting to classroom teachers, labeled by them as "theoretical" and seen as disconnected from critical practice. Refreshingly, we are witnessing changes in the literature on classroom practice as increasing numbers of teachers in schools and in colleges and universities have joined together as collaborative observers/researchers and writers. *Stories from Response-Centered Classrooms: Speaking, Questioning, and Theorizing from the Center of the Action* is an example of this important collaboration at its best.

I like the emphasis in this book on "Stories" as it conveys a personal and situated account of practice. We need such a literature to understand more fully the ongoing complexities and possibilities of teaching and learning, particularly in classrooms that place active learning, real text and performance, actively doing something with what is being learned, at the center. We also need such a literature to understand more fully the power of teacher collaboration. My hope is that the stories will inspire classroom teachers within schools and across schools to join together to reflect on their practice, engage in classroom research and write, becoming in the process the "students of teaching" John Dewey wrote so much about. Students of teaching come together on a regular basis in an effort to enlarge their personal and collective understandings of students' thinking and growth as learners. They are persons who develop and maintain a reflective capacity, becoming in the process clear about their intentions and able to make independent judgments about their classrooms. It is out of such communities of learning that situated writing—from within actual classrooms—will become more common, informing more fully the movement toward reform in the schools.

The six authors of this book—two teacher educators who spend much of their time in classrooms and four middle school teachers—share their stories about how they have translated their beliefs about teaching and learning into practice. They describe, in the process, both their triumphs and their discouragements. Developing what they call "response-centered classrooms" moves them from the center of the classroom, the main actors. They begin to sit alongside their students, bringing about greater equity and more intense learning.

A response-centered approach is defined as

> more than a group of teaching strategies, a curriculum structure, or a classroom-management structure. It is a set of beliefs and practices that guide teachers as they work in their classrooms. Response-centered teaching involves choosing practices that create more equal relationships, that free and enable students to learn, that value humanness and diversity, that acknowledge and affirm what students bring to learning . . .

In the language of contemporary practice, their efforts are aimed at student understanding, that process of internalizing knowledge. They seek active student involvement in interpreting texts, in finding the meaning of narratives, in making connections between written and spoken discourse and their lives. These teachers affirm in a convincing manner that every action or text has embedded in it a genuine response that needs to be valued and respected. In assuming the stance of sitting beside their students, they also provide an example of what it means to be the teacher-coach that Ted Sizer has emphasized within the Coalition of Essential Schools.

The authors ask, "What if you responded to student work as a reader, trying to hear what the author has to say and not reading to evaluate?" Asking such a question pushes these teachers to genuinely engage their students around ideas, around real questions rather than losing their connections to student thought by focusing mostly on form. By taking the stance of a reader, they make meaning the focus, they become an audience. In the process, they model good practice for their students, making clear to them as well that it is a short step from reading each other's work as real readers to reading published literary texts as real readers.

The teachers provide wonderful examples of interactive teaching around texts commonly read in the schools from *To Kill a Mockingbird* to *Guns Up!* The activities that are outlined are imaginative and inspiring. Teachers reading the accounts will see clearly ways of adapting the ideas to their own settings. They will also see that the directions are rooted in a coherent philosophical stance. It is this philosophical stance that provides power to *Stories from Response-Centered Classrooms: Speaking, Questioning, and Theorizing from the Center of the Action,* reaffirming in a practical, understandable manner the critical importance of the teacher and the professionalism inherent in the teacher's role. It also places before us a vision of what is possible for children and their learning when teacher intelligence is engaged and respected. I am pleased the authors have shared their stories.

—Vito Perrone

Preface

We did not start out to write a book. Our story had a modest beginning in 1990 when we agreed to participate in Barb Livdahl's doctoral research. At the time "we" were two experienced junior high English teachers, Joyce Wallman and Janice Anderson; two student teachers, Teresa Krinke and Debra Kramer; a college field instructor with an English education background, Karla Smart; and Barb Livdahl, who was the students' English education instructor. Now "we" are four junior high and middle school teachers and two teacher educators. What has happened to us and what we have learned is so important that we feel compelled to share it with other educators.

For her research Barb chose five books about teaching and asked us to read them and keep a reading log, to discuss them together, and to do whatever seemed appropriate with the ideas and thinking in our classrooms the following fall. We planned a summer retreat where we would get acquainted, discuss the books, and possibly begin initial planning of the fall curriculum. Our discussions were lively and wide-ranging, rich and deep. They were, at the same time, both theoretical and practical. We raised ideas and theories and scrutinized them in the light of the classroom context. Discussions that began about students and classrooms led to theorizing about how new ideas and thinking could "fit" or influence change in classroom life and student behavior.

Late one afternoon we were sitting around the coffee table, tape recorder running, Hershey bar wrappers and Coke cans strewn about, talking about the word *response* and what would happen if response were central to our curriculums. For two days we had spiraled around the question with our stories and experiences as teachers and learners. Suddenly we realized we were talking about a whole way of approaching teaching—a group of beliefs—that would guide our classroom decision making and help us construct learning communities marked by more respectful relationships between students and peers and students and teacher. We named this approach to teaching the response-centered approach.

We were not surprised that it was much easier to envision response-centered teaching in the golden glow of a northwoods log cabin when the intensity of student needs and intentions and the challenges of school structure, colleagues, administrators, and parents were at a distance. Because we know well from personal experience the complexities of schools and classrooms, issues of context are integral to the construction of the response-centered approach and to our continued translation of the theory into practice. Perhaps what we didn't fully realize was the challenge responsive teaching would present to our creativity, intelligence, and self-confidence or the domino effect it would have on all facets of our teaching.

This book is about response-centered teaching and learning. Each of us tells her personal story of translating the shared beliefs into classroom relationships and practices. Our stories are filled with the satisfactions, struggles, and disappointments we have experienced these last several years as we have constructed response-centered learning communities at the middle school, junior high, and college levels.

This book is also about teacher research and collaboration between junior high/middle school and college educators. The knowledge we have created about response-centered teaching and learning is the result of such individual and collaborative classroom research.

We all place a high value on our collaboration. When we began as a collaborative research group, we were all living in the Fargo, North Dakota/Moorhead, Minnesota, area. Now Deb and Teresa live and teach in suburban Minneapolis. Deb teaches seventh-grade English and Teresa teaches eighth-grade reading and language arts. Although Janice and Joyce are still teaching in the same school in Fargo, Janice is now teaching seventh- and eighth-grade English on an interdisciplinary team. Remaining in Moorhead, Karla teaches English education courses in addition to the general education courses and liberal arts course she was teaching at the beginning of our collaboration, and Barb teaches undergraduate and graduate education courses at an Indiana university. Even though we are separated geographically, we continue to explore and collaborate about response-centered teaching.

The wonderful luxury of talking about teaching and learning with others who share a similar belief system and who also love to "talk school" runs up our phone bills and draws us together annually. Our ideas and thinking expand, and our perspectives widen as we support and challenge one another. Most of all, however, we all believe that to have a more complete picture of effective teaching and learning, both K–12 and college educators must contribute their knowledge and experiences.

The traditional research relationship between K–12 and university educators has been structured by a paradigm that is far from collaborative. To avoid the traditional paradigm in which university persons "do" research and "hand" it to K–12 educators to implement, Barb designed the original project as a collaboration. Each of us read and logged our way through the same five books and centered our discussions around this question: What are the implications for the secondary language arts classroom when response is central to the curriculum? It was a "happy surprise" for all that the discussions led to our construction of the response-centered approach.

Geography and the differing research expectations of K–12 schools and colleges have produced conditions that have influenced the nature of our collaboration in the writing of this book. Since we are now situated farther apart geographically, collaboration is more difficult than it was at the beginning of this project. We took this into consideration when we planned the structure of the book. We decided that individuals would write their stories in separate chapters, and we assigned Barb to write Chapter 1, which describes our shared beliefs, and Karla to write the last chapter, which tells what it all means to us by naming themes that stand out for us now and asking questions for the future.

We are concerned that this structure could suggest to the reader that the college authors are the theorists and the secondary teachers are the practitioners. This is not so. We are all practitioners and we are all theorizers. All of us theorized continually throughout the research project, and we continue to theorize as we implement and refine the response-centered practices in our classrooms. The meanings we have constructed from our classroom experiences are evident in what we have selected to narrate and describe in the individual chapters. We see this book as theoretical in every chapter.

The process of writing the first and last chapters is also more collaborative than it may seem. Even though Barb and Karla wrote these chapters, we all contributed ideas and theorizing and participated as readers and revisers. We tend to think of these chapters as "all of us," on the one hand, and "written" by the person whose computer printed them, on the other hand.

We have found that the difference in value placed on the activities of research and writing by colleges and universities as compared to K–12 schools has also influenced the nature of our collaboration. Because these activities are highly valued by colleges and universities, they provide conditions that encourage them. For example, both Karla and Barb receive funding to attend conferences; they also have private offices with telephones and easy access to secretarial help. Therefore it is easier for them to communicate with the other collaborators and publisher. In addition, their more flexible schedules more easily accommodate research and writing. For these logistical reasons, Barb and Karla have coordinated the writing of the book.

This book shares a similar theoretical base with other books and articles about responsive teaching and reader-response literary theory and methodology. It is different, however, in that issues of classroom and school context were integral to the initial construction of the response-centered approach and remain central today as we continue to translate the theory into our practices. We speak, question, and theorize from the center of the action—the classroom itself—where our daily experiences remind us of the powerful personal, social, and political forces that control what is learned and how and why it is taught. We do not ignore the influence of powerful peers, disinterested and disenfranchised students, or kids with an "attitude." Nor do we ignore the skepticism of teacher peers, the questions and expectations of parents and administrators, the mandates of school districts and state boards of education, or our own self-doubts. The understanding that teaching and learning are socially motivated and supported is integral to the approach itself.

A second distinguishing characteristic of the response-centered approach is that it goes beyond reader-response literary theory. While reader-response theory has strongly influenced our thinking, it is only a part of the response-centered approach. In addition to the transactive relationships between readers and texts described by reader-response theory, response-centered classrooms involve more equal, transactive relationships between teacher and students and students and students.

We write this book because we want to add our voices to discussions of effective teaching. We speak with varying years of teaching experience and from a variety of contexts: traditional junior high and middle school structures; disciplinary and interdisciplinary team teaching and solo teaching; undergraduate English education and general secondary education, liberal arts, and graduate education.

We want to describe the response-centered approach to other educators because we have found it to be a way of teaching grounded in sound educational theory that offers students and teachers opportunities for meaningful learning and personal growth. It is also a good fit with current educational trends that value process, community building, and integration. We want to share with other educators our discovery that while translating theory into practice is certainly a messy business, it is also creative and energizing.

We believe that by telling our stories and recording our conversations, we can show what response-centered learning communities look like and how they operate. This is an important addition to the discussions of effective teaching because response-centered learning communities are stimulating, satisfying places for teachers and students to work.

Acknowledgments

We are deeply indebted to all of our students who have helped us to construct response-centered communities and taught us how it is to learn in such communities. Their responses have kept our feet firmly planted on the classroom floor. Special thanks to John Borge for his photographic work and to those students whose work appears in this book: Rita S. Adams, Jane Charpentier, Kimberly Claussen Eastlund, Laila Hollenbeck, Jessica Johnson, Kathy Kentopp, Bethany Lorence Natzke, Thuyet Nguyen, Gressa Rowland, Gretchen Rud, Justin Schermerhorn, Jeff Smenyak, and Eva Stenzel.

We acknowledge our colleagues: Don Arenz, Patricia Carini, Anita de Angelis, Jean Gumpper, Susan Hougan, Affi Ingberg, Pat Schmidt, Cecelia Traugh, Carol Varner, and Susan Wellington. Their questions have required us to think and rethink our ideas and practices; their interest and support have made us continue to think and rethink. Susan Caine Williams deserves special recognition for the significant contribution she made to the construction of the response-centered approach. Susan participated in the summer retreat and Saturday discussions that followed.

We are indebted to Cliff and Beryl Smith, who invited us to Shining Rocks, their Lake Superior retreat, for our summer meetings. The beauty and peacefulness of the northwoods and Lake Superior inspired our thinking and theorizing.

We also acknowledge the support and encouragement provided by the schools in which we have conducted our research: Ben Franklin Junior High, Fargo, North Dakota; Minnetonka Middle School East, Minnetonka, Minnesota; Central Junior High and Sunrise Park Middle School, White Bear Lake, Minnesota; Concordia College, Moorhead, Minnesota; and Valparaiso University, Valparaiso, Indiana. We are particularly grateful to Concordia College for the summer grant that supported our initial research.

Special thanks to Vito Perrone, who has authored the Foreword of this book, and to Sandra Johnson, who has tirelessly transcribed tapes and, along with Lisa Pappas and Andrea Walter, saved us from clerical disaster. We also acknowledge the encouragement and expert guidance of Susan Liddicoat and Jonas Soltis at Teachers College Press throughout the writing and publishing process.

Finally, we are grateful to family members and friends who have supported and encouraged our inquiry and writing: Bruce, Amy, Liza Anderson and Bau Tran; Rick Geiger; Wensley Herbert; Beth, Rich, and Mary Kelly; Larry, Gail, Steve, Kathy, and Greg Kramer; Arlen, Madelyn, Anita, Katy, and Debbie Krinke; Roger Livdahl; George, Marc, and Beth Wallman; Allen and Ashley Bosch, Ilo Leiseth, and the late Alice Underbakke.

CHAPTER 1

Speaking, Questioning, and Theorizing from the Center of the Action

BARBARA SMITH LIVDAHL

Teresa: Respect the students. Respect their responses. Help them to have a part in learning. That's response-centered teaching!

Deb: It makes sense to me. This is how students should feel—nurtured, not oppressed.

Janice: I could never go back again to having students fill in blanks. I could never go back and shut off those voices.

Karla: Response-centered teaching is exhausting, but that kind of exhaustion is energizing also. If what we do is genuine to us and we are constantly growing and changing, it loses that assembly-line kind of feel.

Barb: I like it because it facilitates real learning. Learners experience, or come in contact with, something different; hypothesize about it in terms of their own worlds; and then they do something with it—that's learning.

Joyce: This approach is not revolutionary, it's just logical. It provides for individualism in an untracked classroom. It gives an opportunity to reach the slower student and the student who is curious and bright—without expense, without leaving people out . . .

It was early November, 1990, and the first 11 weeks of school had gone by. We six teacher researchers were reflecting together on our experiences using the response-centered approach in our classrooms. The student teacher–teacher pairs—Deb Kramer and Janice Anderson, and Teresa Krinke and Joyce Wallman—had collaborated on planning and teaching seventh- and ninth-grade English, respectively. Karla Smart and Barb Livdahl had observed in their classrooms as well as used response-centered practices in the college classes they were teaching.

The response-centered approach grew out of our collaborative exploration, which had begun the previous spring when we first gathered as a teacher research group to aid Barb in her doctoral research. Individually we read and logged summaries, questions, and personal responses to the following books: *From Communication to Curriculum* (Barnes, 1992),[1] *Inside High School: The Student's World* (Cusick, 1973), *The English Coalition Conference: Democracy Through Language* (Lloyd-Jones & Lunsford, 1989), *How Porcupines Make Love II: Teaching a Response-Centered Literature Curriculum* (Purves, Rogers, & Soter, 1990), and *Reading Without Nonsense* (Smith, 1985). During a 4-day summer retreat, we discussed the ideas and issues presented in these books in relation to the question: What are the implications for the secondary language arts classroom when response is central to the curriculum? We began to formulate an approach to teaching that we called a "response-centered approach." Teresa and Joyce and Deb and Janice began to construct response-centered learning activities for the fall semester. During the fall, as we all taught, journaled, and discussed, and as Karla and Barb observed in the classrooms, we refined, redefined, and enlarged the germ of the approach.

Our summer retreat had given us a rare opportunity to become immersed in the discussion of teaching and learning. We brought to these discussions our knowledge of the English discipline and the materials and methods of teaching English, our own experiences as teachers and learners, our understanding of adolescents and the social context of the school, and our own beliefs about the purposes of education and what it is to be human.

It became clear early in our discussions that we share many similar values as well. For example, we all place high value on persons, and the aims we share for our students are wrapped up in their humanness. Of course, we want them to possess the skills of reading, writing, speaking, listening, and thinking. But these are the basics. We have more in mind for them. We want them to read, write, speak, listen, and think so that they can express themselves effectively and their voices will be heard. We want them to read and enjoy literature

---

1. We read the 1975 first edition, but subsequent quotations are from the 1992 second edition.

so that their understanding of themselves and others will be enlarged and their enjoyment of beauty and well-expressed ideas sharpened. We believe there is more to be accomplished than learning skills and acquiring knowledge. Therefore we want to establish classroom communities in which respect for individuals is paramount and diversity is celebrated so that the students' self-esteem and confidence are strengthened and they will be thoughtful, creative, and critically reflective citizens.

WHAT DO WE MEAN BY RESPONSE?

Early in our retreat discussions we realized that we needed to understand the meanings each of us held for *response,* a key word in the focus question. We realized that whether or not our meanings, assumptions, and questions are made explicit, teachers and students all act upon their understandings of the word. The meanings teachers attribute to response undergird teaching practice and touch students' lives. To uncover these meanings required more than a dictionary.

Through the use of the reflection process developed by Patricia Carini, we reflected on our ideas, meanings, memories, and associations around the words *talk, conversation,* and *response.* Traugh (1985) offers this description of Carini's reflection process:

> As an activity, a reflection is deceptively simple. People are asked to think about and write down the meanings, images, and conditions surrounding their use of a word or phrase. The results of the process are less easily described. What people write in a reflection is more than "what they think" in the conventional sense. What they write, and then share orally, includes associations, images, metaphors, and feelings. There are few logical definitions or explanations. Each reflection varies from person to person, but they typically take on a non-discursive or non-expository form. As individuals share their thoughts about the word in question, patterns emerge. The patterns, with their collective base, form beginning points for understanding larger, cultural and social meanings, or what some social scientists term intersubjective meanings. Beginning patterns become a base for further study, describing themes, contrasts, and ideas of potential importance. (p. 85)

Each of us reflected individually on the word *response.* Because the reflection process is a valuable strategy in response-centered teaching, we decided to include Deb's individual reflection as an example to show how Carini's process works (see Figure 1.1).

Figure 1.1. Deb Geiger's reflection on the word *response*.

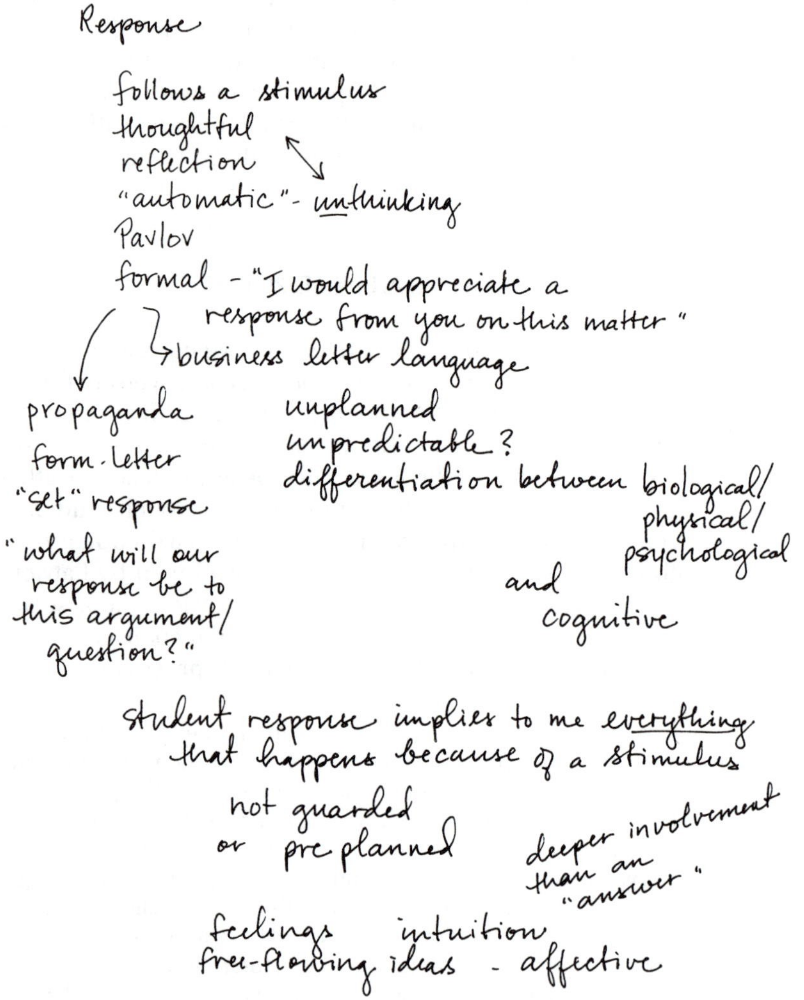

Response

follows a stimulus
thoughtful
reflection
"automatic" - unthinking
Pavlov
formal - "I would appreciate a
      response from you on this matter "
        ↳ business letter language

propaganda   unplanned
form-letter   unpredictable?
"set" response   differentiation between biological/
                                          physical/
"what will our   psychological
response be to   and
this argument/   cognitive
question?"

student response implies to me everything
    that happens because of a stimulus
        not guarded
      or preplanned   deeper involvement
                          than an
                          "answer"
    feelings   intuition
    free-flowing ideas - affective

After generating words, phrases, images, and ideas to express our individual understandings of the word *response,* we took turns describing the lists and elaborating ideas. Our purpose was to develop fullness and range in understanding response. We specifically did not limit ourselves to the context of schooling while reflecting. The word did not elicit just one impression, nor did it yield a single connotative meaning. Since reflection summaries attempt to pattern or group ideas and to include or represent all ideas listed or talked about in the process of reflection, they have a free, poetic form. We include Karla's summary of our reflections on *response* both as an example and to uncover the range of ideas and thinking involved in responding:

> Response is wide-ranging. It is an essential, universal process or rhythm. Every existence, every presence, every event in creation produces response in the world. Response is the way of the ecosystem, the life of the environment. Similarly, response is essential to humanness. It is what humans do as well as what they need and seek.
>
> Response can be thoughtful or impulsive, planned or spontaneous, expected or surprising, intuitive, instinctual, interpretive, exploratory, active or passive. Response can be withheld, making no response a response. Response can be recursive. A pebble tossed into a pond produces widening rings. A response can make connections among ideas, events, or persons and it can predict further possibility or additional response. One pattern found in nature, among persons, and with machinery or technology is: stimulus followed by response. However, another pattern is: response followed by response, followed by response.
>
> Just as the meanings we ascribe to response vary with contexts, so too the meanings we attach to no response. Given no response, an idea or being or relationship may be thought of as closed, or exhausted, or dead. To receive, or even to perceive, no response may be understood as a relief or an insult, a benefit or a loss—and on through the full range of cognitive and emotional dimensions of human interpretations.
>
> Response is part of human expression and communication. We respond to movies, books, art, letters. We respond to expressions of the human creative impulse. We respond to nature, sending food or clothing and preparing sandbags in response to natural disaster. We respond to each other—to tragedy, to argument, to love, to creative expression, to authority, or to vulnerability. Response may be something automatic, something conditioned like Pavlov and his dog reveal. And yet we regard response as something to call out, prompt or provoke, invite, motivate, nurture. We regard response as something to release or, by contrast, as something to withhold.
>
> Response is often understood in terms of time. A phrase such as "before I could respond" becomes part of the story of a

car accident. Following a film or gallery visit, or before a decision or choice is to be made, a phrase such as "I'll have to think
about that" is heard. The exchange of stimulus and response,
understood philosophically, relates stimulus with the responder's perception of the past, the present, and the future. Humans
often feel a response needs to be immediate or instantaneous.
Press the button, get a response. Yet response often implies a
deeper involvement on the part of the responder than does, for
example, an answer.

In addition to taking time, a response often involves emotion. We may expect response to be personal, wondering how
another will feel. Questions such as "How does it make you
feel?" or "How do you respond to that?" regard the person as
well as the response. As responders, we may be eager or hesi-
tant. We may protect ourselves by not responding unless asked,
or we may eagerly ask, "Is it my turn now?"

The baggage, or world view, we carry influences our response, just as it influences our understanding of stimulus.
Value is given to a response. Judgment, whether positive or negative, may be implied or stated in the response we receive to our
response—"Is that your only response?" Or the feedback related
to our response may be supporting and validating.

We may find it difficult to separate ourselves from the response received to our responses. We may change or extinguish
behavior, change or question opinion and belief in response to
the responses we receive. We may find ourselves fully involved
in the push–pull rhythm of perceiving and responding. Listeners
or readers may discover a speaker or writer's world meeting their
own. They may fill in gaps, they may interrupt, or question, or
elaborate ideas as their world view meets another's.

These broad and collective thoughts widened the base for our
understanding of the response-centered approach we were articulat-
ing, for the choices we made in classrooms to offer students opportunities to respond, and for our reception and understanding of the
responses—the meanings—students were to make.

WHAT IS THE RESPONSE-CENTERED APPROACH?

It is difficult to describe the response-centered approach because it
is more than a group of teaching strategies, a curriculum structure,

or a classroom-management scheme. It is a set of beliefs and practices that guide teachers as they work in their classrooms. Response-centered teaching involves choosing practices that create more equal relationships, that free and enable students to learn, that value humanness and diversity, that acknowledge and affirm what students bring to learning, and that nurture students' development. At the center of the response-centered approach is an interaction pattern characterized by response—the response of students to teachers, teachers to students, and students to students, and both students and teachers to published and student-generated and teacher-generated texts.

The instructions and student responses recorded from the following learning activity illustrate what response-centered teaching looked like in Janice and Deb's classroom at the end of the first week of a unit on family (see also Chapters 5 and 6).

At the end of a week in which the seventh-grade students had read "One-Shot Finch," a chapter from *To Kill a Mockingbird* by Harper Lee,[2] and the poem "Those Winter Sundays" by Robert Hayden in their literature anthology (*Adventures for Readers,* 1979), Janice and Deb gave students the following instructions: "Using all of the knowledge we've produced this week around the word *family* and our impressions of fathers or male leaders in our lives, respond to the story and/or poem we've read." Here are a few of the students' unedited responses:

I never knew you could get so much out of such little writing and you could tell so much of the way the poet was feeling when he/she wrote the poem. I guess I thought of poems as just some words put together that people like to read. I never really knew why they liked reading them.

I think that the poem is kind of weird, not at all like the funny ones I like to read by people like Shel Silverstein and Jack Prelutsky. I don't quite think that it goes along with some of the activities that we've done already because it is not really a happy poem. I didn't quite understand some parts like "fear the chronic angers of that house" and "love's austere and lonely offices." It wasn't too bad, but it isn't the type of poem that I like to read. Poems like this are sort of like abstract art; you have to look at it

---

2. Bibliographic information on literature selections mentioned in the text is provided at the end of each chapter.

over and over again before you get the idea that the artist was trying to make, and even then you might have to sort of guess what the artist is trying to say: just the same way as I have to read this poem over and over again to really understand it. I guess I just prefer more simple things.

This poem leaves lots of questions unanswered. Some poems are like that. It's like a story written without all the facts. YOU must make up the end. YOU must figure out all the answers. Most of the answers cannot be figured out alone though. You must add imagination. This poem makes me think and probably makes lots of others think. I do not personally enjoy poems that much. I like long stories better that answer all your questions at the end. Poems are beautifully written, but some people look at what's inside, not the package. Of course, I do agree poems have a lot of content. I think of them more as beautifully written.

When we talked about the most important male in our family, It was good. Because my parents are devoorced And its important to wright about your father, when your parent are divoorced. My dad is moving to Floridi and I need the memorys about him, because he will be moving far away. he will send us some arline tikit to so we can visit him.

These student responses are truly remarkable. They demonstrate a high level of cognitive and emotional involvement. Students took full advantage of the freedom to define the problem from the perspectives of their own knowledge, beliefs, current situations, and intentions, and to form their answers to fit their own purposes. For example, the first writer wrote about the form of a poem. It was as if she hadn't considered poetry as a form of human expression before. This is a genuinely important discovery.

The second writer responded to the specific poem "Those Winter Sundays." His claim to "prefer simple things" is surely undermined by his complex response. He compared "Those Winter Sundays" to the funny poems of Shel Silverstein and Jack Prelutsky that he likes to read, and it came up "weird." He compared the unhappy mood of the poem with the happy mood of the other activities of the week, and it didn't fit. He quoted the parts of the poem that he didn't understand, and he thought about how he had read them over and over, trying to make sense of them in the same way he looks at abstract art over and over again as he tries to make sense of it.

The third writer responded to the reading of poems as compared to the reading of stories. She has a clear sense of what the reader has to do to read a poem like "Those Winter Sundays." She notes that the reader must not only "make up the end" and "figure out all the answers," but also use her imagination. On the other hand, she appreciates poetry because it makes her think and it's "beautifully written." After exploring her feelings about poetry and comparing reading poetry with reading long stories, she concludes that she "personally [doesn't] enjoy poems that much."

The last writer responded to one of the activities of the week, which was to write about the most important male in your life. He connected with what is undoubtedly uppermost in his mind at the moment—his father's moving away and his need to have "memorys" about him. He shows his wisdom when he says it is important to "wright about your father, when your parent are divoorced" and he assures himself that he will not forget his father, and his father will not forget him, with his mention of the "arline tikit." The assignment offered him the opportunity to write about his fears, to make them "available to introspection and revision" (Barnes, 1992, p. 19) so that he could make sense of them.

Several instructional options had been open to Janice and Deb at the end of the first week of this 6-week literature unit centered on the theme of family relationships. For example, since this was only the end of the first week of the unit, one option would have been to move on without any summary activity with the belief that the succeeding literature selections would expand students' understanding. Other options would have been to give a true–false or matching quiz on the titles, authors, and characters of the selections read, to ask students to write a brief explanation of the meanings of each selection, or to have a class discussion using specific questions such as, "What did line 5 mean?" or "Why did the children in the story reject their father?" A more open option would have been to allow students to respond in any way they chose.

The instructions Janice and Deb formulated for this writing illustrate several response-centered practices. First, they credited their seventh-graders with having "created knowledge" about the word *family.* Second, they validated students' "impressions of fathers and male leaders in their lives." And third, instead of asking students to answer specific questions about the events or interpretation of the selections, they asked them to pull together their own knowledge and impressions and to "respond."

Their instructions also set up conditions for school learning similar to those that help children learn outside of school. For example, the students were free to define their own "problems" to explore and given the encouragement to imagine and shape their own solutions. Being able to recognize a problem and imagine it solved is basic to learning (Boomer, 1987). The conditions they set also encouraged students to make connections to their own past knowledge, current experiences, and future meanings by exploring, hypothesizing, predicting, and testing the hypothesis just as they would with an outside-of-school problem. Very often solving school problems requires memorizing and manipulating facts and information rather than making connections. This approach is in contrast to more common questioning practices in which the question defines both the problem and the shape of the answer.

The teachers' instructions imply their understanding that language learning is transactive—that the students' interpretations of the past week's experiences will transact with their interpretations of the story or poem and that in that transaction new knowledge will be formulated. There will, therefore, not be one "right answer," but many diverse interpretations.

WHAT ARE THE ASSUMPTIONS
BASIC TO THE RESPONSE-CENTERED APPROACH?

Through our reading and discussion of the research literature, we identified the following assumptions as the foundations of the response-centered approach to teaching and learning:

1. Learning is a constructive process in which learners make sense of their environments by experiencing, exploring, hypothesizing, predicting, testing, and synthesizing.
2. Language is integral to the learning process.
3. Learning occurs in the social context.

Because it is important to understand these beliefs, which undergird the response-centered practices described in this book, I will discuss each of them more fully.

Learning Is a Constructive Process

The work of psychologists, psycholinguists, and educational theorists has led to a view of learning as a constructive process. Smith

(1985) relates schema theory to children's learning, particularly to their learning to read. He believes that everyone has a "theory of the world" (p. 73) in his or her head and that the theory is the "root" of all learning. Smith calls the person's picture of the world a theory to indicate that the brain is not filled with isolated bits of knowledge or beliefs, but that the knowledge and beliefs are integrated into complex systems, or schemata. Infants and young children construct their theories of the world at the same time they learn oral language. They accomplish this by hypothesizing, predicting, and testing new experiences or information as they make sense of their environments. Martin (1988) points to children's oral language learning as a model for all learning.

This same process of learning is evident in Dewey's (1916/1944) essential elements of the process of reflective thinking. According to Dewey, reflective thinking begins with doubts and confusion raised by an experience and proceeds to a more settled state of mind as the thinker comes to terms with the experiences that initially raised the doubts and confusion.

Rosenblatt (1978) implies a constructive learning process in her literary response theory when she suggests that readers transact with text, and in the transaction create a new text. She uses the word *transact* to indicate that the meaning resides in both the text and the reader and that in the transaction, reader and text influence each other as the new text is constructed.

Harste, Woodward, and Burke (1984) discuss three models of learning, two of which are constructive: the transactive and the cognitive models. The third model, which is not constructive, is the behavioral model. The response-centered approach can be characterized as transactive because the process of constructing relationships and the act of responding are transactive processes. For example, we believe that the meanings (theories of the world) students bring to the classroom transact with the new experience and in the process new knowledge or understanding is created.

The transactive model is in contrast with the behavioral model of learning in which learning is said to be the result of the environment acting on the learner; therefore, if there are problems in learning, they rest in the environment, not in the learner. The learner is passive, a receiver of knowledge rather than a constructor of knowledge. For example, those individuals who believe that people learn to write by first mastering English grammar and usage are suggesting that a particular environment—one in which students are drilled in grammar and punctuation skills, for example—will be the best place for students to become skillful writers. In other words, people holding this view assume that learning to write effectively is best accomplished by the step-by-step mastering of subskills.

In contrast to the behavioral model in which the meanings rest in the environment, the cognitive model assumes that meanings rest in the learner, in those "assimilative schemas available in the head of the language user" (Harste et al., 1984, p. 58). Harste and colleagues argue that by ignoring the influence of the environment, the cognitive model fails to explain why children tend to develop the language of their interpretive communities. Both the cognitive and transactive models describe learning as a constructive process. However, the transactive model acknowledges the importance of both the learner and the environment.

Language Is Integral to Learning

Learners use language as they construct meanings and also to communicate their meanings to others. Bruner (1986) and Britton (1970) point out that learners naturally use language as they bring order to their environments. In order to construct knowledge, students must make connections among what they already know, the new knowledge and experiences being presented to them, and the future meanings of these experiences.

Barnes (1992) suggests that talking and writing are the major means by which learners in school make these connections. For example, talking and writing help students relate "school knowledge," which Barnes defines as that knowledge which someone else presents, with "action knowledge," which he defines as that knowledge which they have already assimilated and out of which their actions and behaviors flow. Writing and talking also "provide the means of testing out school knowledge against the action knowledge" (p. 82). Unless "school knowledge" is incorporated in some way into what students believe, it will remain "school knowledge," the property of someone else, and be virtually useless.

Many contemporary educational researchers have explored and theorized about how this view of learning influences educational practice. The extensive body of research related to writing process, whole language, the use of talking and writing to learn, and responsive teaching is based on a constructive view of learning. For example, writing process research has provided classroom practices that encourage the type of writing activities that help students make connections. Elbow (1973) proposed the idea that instead of the traditional "meaning-into-language" view of writing, writers should begin writing and the meaning will evolve. Murray (1985) argues that "meaning is not thought up and then written down. The act of writing is an act of thought" (p. 3). Their theories have lead to such writing-to-learn practices as free writing and journaling, which can be important modes of response for students.

Learning Occurs in the Social Context

While it is true that hypothesizing, testing, and reframing are acts of individuals, individuals are motivated to perform these acts as they live in society (Barnes, 1992; Dewey, 1916/1944; Pradl, 1988). Bruner (1986) writes that learning is a "communal activity, a sharing of the culture" (p. 123), and Vygotsky (1978) hypothesizes that as children develop "an interpersonal process is transformed into an intra-personal one. Every function in the child's personal development appears twice, the first on the social level and later on the individual level" (p. 57).

Sociolinguists like Edwards and Westgate (1987) and Halliday (1978) point out that in addition to being a catalyst for learning and for providing learners the support of peers, teachers, and other adults, the social context influences what can and does occur in the classroom. In other words, it has the potential to limit or enhance the students' opportunity to use their language for learning, thus controlling how and what they learn. Teachers, together with students, establish the implicit rules for who can talk and what they can say, who asks the questions and how they should be answered, and who makes the decisions and how they should be accepted.

Perhaps the most powerful influences on classroom learning are the interaction patterns that exist between students. Ethnographer Cusick (1973) found that school is a friendship-based society. The most important value for students is being accepted by peers, not learning. Popular students can influence the social context positively or negatively; either way they set the standards for who talks and what is or isn't said or done. Students will do whatever is necessary to preserve their time and opportunities to nurture and maintain their friendships.

The traditional pattern of communication in the classroom places the teacher as the expert and the students as passive receivers of knowledge. These traditional patterns are embodied in the common classroom discourse patterns of "known-information" questions and "question–answer–evaluation/feedback sequences." A known-information question is one to which the teacher already knows the answer. Teachers ask these questions to test the knowledge of the students.

The question–answer–evaluation/feedback sequence begins with the teacher asking a question, then the student answering the question, and then the teacher evaluating the student's answer. This pattern of exchange is used so frequently by teachers that many have called it the essential teaching exchange. Because teachers have every third turn, this sequence allows them to control the discussion and steer it in a predetermined direction. Both of these patterns place a heavy burden on students because they must not only determine what answer the teacher is looking for, but also be prepared to have their answers evaluated. The clearly marked roles, teacher as expert and student as ignorant, are evident in these common patterns.

Teachers also most commonly assume the expert role as they read and evaluate students' written and oral work. Pradl (1988) cites an incident in which he read a paper to a group of teachers who were discussing the problems teachers face when teaching writing to students whose writing skills are below expectations. The paper was written by a 21-year-old woman who only recently had come to the United States from Taiwan. He asked the teachers what questions they would like to ask the author. With only a few exceptions, their responses concentrated on form errors or potential process problems. Pradl wrote that he was trying to point out that here was a "real speaking person behind this paper, a person who deserved listening to" (p. 46). In assuming the expert, evaluator role, these teachers became separated from the writer as a person.

Just as these unequal interaction patterns can have a negative effect on students' learning, so more equal and respectful relationships can enhance learning. Therefore we have worked together with our students to construct classroom contexts in which interaction patterns between students and their peers and between students and us increase the amount of student talk and the range of language our students can use. We have also searched for ways to help our students respect themselves and their peers as learners and as valued persons. Our classroom experience has convinced us that the classroom social system/communication system is a critical component in how and what students learn.

HOW DO THESE ASSUMPTIONS INFLUENCE CLASSROOM PRACTICE?

As we translated these three assumptions into classroom practices, it became clear to us that they implied a different social structure and communication system from the traditional classroom. When we acknowledge that students enter the classroom as knowledgeable and capable learners and that learning is a constructive process, we can no longer see ourselves as the experts or students as the ignorant recipients of knowledge. We can no longer see ourselves as transmitters of knowledge to students. Instead, we need to design teaching practices that facilitate the students' use of their natural learning processes and equalize classroom relationships. Both teachers and students must acknowledge and respect each other as knowers and learners, and the classroom discourse patterns must reflect this more equal relationship.

Because we believe that language is integral to learning, we structure plentiful occasions for reflective and exploratory talk and writing. Since we believe that learning occurs in the social context and that the social context is both a catalyst for learning and a necessary support for the learner's development, we structure the classroom around challenging and worthy ideas and explorations, and provide opportunities for students to interact with us and with their peers as they explore and shape new meanings. Students and teachers together create a classroom communication system/social structure that provides every learner the conditions for using his or her language for learning.

LITERATURE SELECTIONS

Adventures for readers (Book 1, Heritage Edition). (1979). New York: Harcourt Brace Jovanvich.

Hayden, Robert. (1979). Those winter Sundays. In *Adventures for readers* (Book 1, Heritage Edition; p. 108). New York: Harcourt Brace Jovanovich.

Lee, Harper. (1960). One-shot Finch from *To kill a mockingbird*. In *Adventures for readers* (Book 1, Heritage Edition; pp. 98–106). New York: Harcourt Brace Jovanovich.

CHAPTER 2

Any More Questions?
I Certainly Hope So

BARBARA SMITH LIVDAHL

When people ask me what I do, I quickly respond, "I am a teacher."
But I am also a researcher and a scholar. I can't separate the two. For
me teaching and inquiry are intertwined. My questions have shaped
my daily teaching and even my career changes. For example, when
a few of my high school English students still couldn't read effectively, even after good instruction, I searched for answers in my
classrooms, at conferences, in journals, and through college
coursework on learning disabilities. Although I didn't find *the one*
answer to why, I have learned numerous ways to help students with
disabilities, and along the way I also earned a master's degree in
special education.

Classroom experiences continually suggest new questions to me.
The question that inspired this collaborative study—What are the
implications for the secondary classroom when response is central
to the curriculum?—grew out of my experiences as a classroom
teacher and my students' questions.

BEGINNING ENCOUNTERS WITH RESPONSE

My first encounter with response came in 1988 when I was teaching
composition to first-year college students. One day my colleague
Don Arenz said, "Here's one to think about, Barb. What do you think
would happen if you read your students' papers like a real reader?"

"Real reader? What do you mean by that?" I countered.

"I mean like you read magazine articles and books," he replied, "not reading to evaluate, but actually reading to hear what the author has to say."

That certainly started me thinking. I asked Don more questions; I read books and articles he suggested; I observed his classroom; and finally, I began responding to students' papers as a reader and not an evaluator. What a change it made! My students began to write more, and their voices became lively and passionate. I looked forward to reading their papers, and they looked forward to reading my comments.

I shared these experiences with the preservice teachers taking the English Methods course I was teaching. We read and discussed Peter Elbow's (1981) chapters on criterion-based and reader-based response to writing. We practiced responding to each other's papers as "real" readers. We read Nancie Atwell's *In the Middle* (1987) and discussed how she responded to students in reading and writing workshops.

It was but a small leap from reading students' writings as a real reader to reading literary texts as a real reader. It seems strange to suggest that readers read literary texts otherwise, but students of literature often slip into the "reading as a critic" mode, and more seriously, English majors preparing to be secondary teachers often slip into expecting their students to read as critics, too. Unfortunately, what this often leads to in the literature classroom is a series of discussions or lectures in which the teacher tells students what the critics say about the selection in question. Students begin to wonder where those ideas came from and to think of themselves as poor readers and literature as irrelevant.

When we discussed teaching literature, we read Rosenblatt (1978), Probst (1988), and others who write about reading as a process in which readers construct meanings in transaction with the text. English education students realized that if each classroom reader created a new meaning from the text, discussions could no longer center on a single meaning. Would there be "wrong" meanings? Would class discussions have any substance?

We decided that we should experience responding to literature ourselves. We read together a short poem and wrote individually about what the words said to us. Then we shared our responses in small groups. When describing their small-group discussions to the entire class, students expressed surprise at the variety of interpretations in their groups. They had found themselves asking each other where they had gotten "that" idea and returning to the text again and again for answers. I asked students what they wanted to do next.

They asked to write again, thinking that they would likely come closer to agreement on the meaning of this short poem. However, we were astonished to find that this writing only brought more questions about the language, the images, and the poet's intentions. It became clear to us that responding followed by discussion of responses could definitely lead to substantive literary discussions. These discussions would be different from traditional teacher-led discussions because they would be driven by the reader's own need to make sense of the selection. We were hooked.

After each of these experiences we critiqued what happened to us individually and as a group. The more the students and I questioned and experimented, the more convinced we became of the value of authentic response in teaching both composition and literature. We found that authentic response increased our interest and desire to read and write. We felt respected because we were encouraged to construct our own meanings, and our meanings were valued. Our confidence as learners and teachers increased, and response promised more respectful, democratic relationships in the classroom. This was what we wanted to have happen in our classrooms.

But, the students and I asked, what would happen in "real" secondary classrooms? Would secondary students respond? Could they construct meanings from text? After all, we were all English majors. Would secondary students even read a selection without the structure of study guides, reading quizzes, and teacher-led discussions?

RESPONSE IN "REAL" SECONDARY CLASSROOMS

That's when I went to Joyce and asked her if she would be interested in collaborating on a study of what ninth-grade English students would do when asked to respond to a book. I explained to her how we were talking about response in the English Methods class and shared our questions. After a structured study of *Romeo and Juliet,* Joyce was eager to offer her students something different, so she and I constructed a unit using *Guns Up!,* a book about the Vietnam War written by Johnnie Clark (1984). As Joyce explains in Chapter 3, what we found astonished us. Students persistently and eagerly worked to make sense of the characters' experiences and of the Vietnam War itself. Out of their own curiosity and interest, they probed the author's choices of language and events. These students convinced us that given the opportunity to respond, they could, and would, make their own meanings from texts such as *Guns Up!* [See Livdahl (1993), for a full description of this study.]

Although these students clearly demonstrated that they could respond to text and that responding encouraged them to ask their own questions and search out their own meanings, there were so many more questions. What conditions were necessary for successful responding? How can we teachers provide those conditions? What would happen if responding were central to the entire classroom curriculum, not just a book unit? This last question became the question that focused my doctoral research and, thus, in 1990 the collaborative inquiry of the authors of this book.

DIFFICULTIES AND DILEMMAS OF USING RESPONSE-CENTERED PRACTICES

I found that it was a lot easier to talk about response and its benefits than to actually practice responsive teaching in my composition classes. In the first place, I didn't have teacher models from my own experience as a student to fall back on. Fortunately, Don had learned how to incorporate response in his composition classes, and he willingly shared his ideas with me. We struggled together with ways to increase students' ownership of the literature component of the course. Secondly, the English Department had set specific guidelines for the emphases of the three first-year composition courses: introductory composition, oral discourse, and research writing. The guidelines specified, for example, that students were to learn to write clear and concise sentences and effective paragraphs; various types of essays, such as descriptive, comparative, and persuasive; and a research paper. Also, they were to learn effective oral communication skills, including presenting various types of speeches, one of which was a persuasive speech.

I struggled continually with these composition guidelines. I was convinced that by responding to students and allowing their responses to guide the curriculum, my students would emerge from the year of discourse more effective writers and speakers, but I wasn't so sure they would be able to demonstrate the specific knowledge required by the guidelines. And there was a certain wisdom in the guidelines, too, as well as my responsibility to the discipline, my English Department colleagues, and my colleagues in other departments who depended on us to teach students how to write the various types of essays necessary to succeed in the college classroom.

For me this is the central conflict inherent in teaching responsively. When I provide the conditions for students to use their own language, current knowledge, and learning skills to learn the content of the classroom, their own curiosity and intentions may take them in a different direction from the centrally planned curriculum expectations. Also, such learning takes more classroom time than simply presenting the expected curriculum knowledge via teacher-prepared study guides and tests and teacher-led discussions and lectures. I worry that students might learn to think about ideas, to solve problems, and to apply information, but not acquire a broad enough base of content facts and information.

Perhaps the question is whether to focus on the teaching or the learning. When I focus on students' learning, I can't ensure that we will "cover" all the material expected by succeeding instructors or specified in the curriculum. When I focus on the teaching, I can be sure that at least I have "covered" the required material, but I am not convinced that students have learned it, and I worry that they may consider learning drudgery and school knowledge irrelevant. After all, teaching doesn't equal learning, and shouldn't the teacher's job be to "uncover" material rather than to "cover" it?

The teachers who take the graduate education courses I teach voice the same concerns. They talk of the pressures of teaching to high-stakes, state-mandated achievement tests; the impossibility of "covering" the history of the world in one year or American literature from the colonial period to today in one semester; the need to "cover" so much math or science to prepare students for the next grade; and the importance placed on grades by students, parents, and school administrators. This focus on grades affects the curriculum because it causes teachers to restrict what they teach to what can be graded. They have struggled daily with the question "What's best for my kids?" long before we begin our discussions.

This conflict proved to be an even greater struggle for me when I taught teacher education courses. I believe that I must model responsive teaching practices in my classroom if I want prospective teachers to teach responsively. How can I do that and make sure students know various management strategies, how to write lesson plans, and are acquainted with the theorists and practices that make them literate in the field of education? How can I prepare them to focus on their students' learning amidst the pressures of stated curriculums, students' and parents' expectations, and the pressures of school structures?

Again and again I ask myself if I have done my students a

disservice if they leave my teacher education classrooms with a belief in response-centered teaching and a valuing of classroom practices that will likely place them in conflict with traditional practice. The answer is always the same. It's worth the risk. I cannot ignore the sound research that compels me to believe the assumptions that undergird response-centered teaching. I cannot ignore the persistent drive to make sense of the Vietnam era by the ninth-graders in Joyce's classroom, the liveliness and clarity of student writers' voices in the written texts of my college composition students, or the excitement of education students as they envision new ways of teaching the knowledgeable and capable learners who will people their classrooms. I cannot ignore the satisfaction of teaching in a classroom characterized by respect and more equal relationships.

CREATING A RESPONSE-CENTERED TEACHER EDUCATION CLASSROOM

I believe teachers must provide students with the conditions necessary for them to learn, and that if there is ever to be any reform in education, it will begin with individual teachers. Therefore, now that I teach a full range of education courses, I do everything in my power and understanding to help preservice teachers to develop knowledge of the assumptions undergirding response-centered teaching, to learn practices that help them construct response-centered classrooms, and to convince them that such classrooms provide the conditions for students to learn and that students' learning should be the most important goal of education.

In addition, I believe that I need to help education students develop a philosophy of teaching based on the assumptions of response-centered teaching. This philosophy can guide their planning and on-the-spot decision making. It can give them confidence as they respond to colleagues' and students' questions about their pedagogical choices. Without an articulated set of beliefs, they may find themselves simply "fighting fires," or reacting rather than acting.

Students tell me that most of their previous educational experiences, especially those at the college level, have been with traditional and behavioristic approaches and hierarchical relationships. Before they enter the student teaching semester in our program, however, they have been challenged to think about learning as a constructive process in their educational psychology course. In the content reading course they have discussed reading as a process of constructing meaning in transaction with text and have planned and taught minilessons that aim to help secondary students transact effectively with text.

Yet when these prospective teachers plan the first lessons in my course "Principles and General Methods of Teaching in the Secondary School," they often fall back on those traditional patterns and relationships with which they are so familiar—lectures and teacher-directed discussions. Their previous classroom experiences continue to influence their pedagogical choices despite discussions of a new view of knowledge and student–teacher relationships.

To help students change or enlarge their existing philosophies of teaching and learning requires more than just talking about new ways of thinking and behaving or seeing deficiencies in their existing beliefs. Students must experience for themselves the benefits of learning in a response-centered learning community.

Personal experience seems to be a key element in whether teachers change and enlarge their perspectives. Through their daily classroom experiences, teachers have learned which practices work with which students. When their practices are challenged by theory, often their experience-proven practices win out. This dilemma is evident in the journal of an experienced teacher in a graduate course on writing research. "I just can't decide which information source I should trust," she wrote, "research studies like the ones we're studying or my own experience as a teacher" (Marshall, 1988, p. 2).

To give preservice teachers response-centered learning experiences, students and I must construct a communication system/social structure marked by respect and more equal relationships, and I must model response-centered teaching practices.

I have structured "Principles and General Methods" to provide such experiences. For example, we sit in a circle so that we can make eye contact with one another when we talk. The circle also promotes more equal teacher–student and student–student relationships and the natural turn-taking of conversations because it removes the teacher from the focal point of the discussion. An oval or U shape or a big desk among regular desks signals to students that the teacher is still the discussion manager: All responses will go through her and she will have every third turn in the conversation. Students who have spent most of their classroom time sitting in rows and participating in teacher-led discussions need to experience circle discussions in order to see the change in relationships and the quality of discussion they bring about.

We begin this course by discussing our images of teaching and learning. In groups students draw pictures of secondary classrooms and explain the structure to the class. We talk about behavioral, cognitive, and transactive approaches to learning. We read and discuss "Zen and the Art of Burglary" by Wu-tsu Fa-yen (1989), in which a father teaches his son how to be a burglar by locking him in a chest and then waking up the homeowners, leaving the son to figure his way out of this difficult situation. The roles of teachers and learners come into sharp focus as we discuss this selection. We also read the excerpt from Harper Lee's *To Kill a Mockingbird* (1960) that describes Scout's first day of school. Scout's teacher is dismayed that Scout already knows how to read and write cursive, and Scout reports, "Miss Caroline told me to tell my father not to teach me anymore, it would interfere with my reading" (p. 22). This selection opens discussions of the knowledge and belief systems that students have constructed and that they bring to learning and also of implicit and explicit curriculums.

The way we read and discuss *Small Victories,* the story of urban English teacher Jessica Siegel, written by journalist S. G. Freedman (1990), also encourages individual experiencing and responding. I assign large chunks of reading and ask students to complete a one-pager over the reading. To prepare a one-pager, students draw a visual representation, select two quotes, and write an interpretive statement or comment after having read the selection.

I learned about one-pagers from Gabrielle Rico in her presentation at a National Council of Teachers of English meeting (1991a). Rico, author of *Pain and Possibility: Writing Your Way Through Personal Crisis* (1991b) and *Writing the Natural Way* (1983), suggested that when words and images combine, both sides of the brain are involved in the reading process. In her words, "the brain takes over," empowering the learner to see patterns and clusters of ideas. Students report that as they read, they constantly think about which quotes to choose and what visual element will express their thinking.

Since there are no worksheets with teacher questions that focus students' reading on teacher-selected events, students are free to focus on what is important to them. Jeff Smenyak describes the value of one-pagers for him:

I found the one-pagers extremely helpful in drawing my ideas together. So many times, after reading something, I have not reflected on what was read. It had never dawned on me how important reflective writing was. By drawing our visual, I was able to put into perspective what I wanted to say.

One-pagers completed by Bethany Lorence Natzke and Jeff Smenyak, Figures 2.1 and 2.2, show what was significant to them as they read.

We use these one-pagers as the basis for the daily class discussions about *Small Victories.* As a result, issues of importance to students become the focus of the discussions. I divide students into small groups and suggest that students each take 5 minutes to share their one-pagers with their groups. Small-group discussions are lively and substantive because they are framed by meanings individual students have already shaped as they constructed their one-pagers. Discussions extend students' experiences with the text as peers point out quotes and explain their visual elements. When small groups report to the whole class, students often express surprise at how many issues surface and the variety of connections individuals have made.

When we have finished reading the book, I ask students to make a portfolio of all their one-pagers and write a reflection on what they have learned from the book and how the one-pager process worked for them. Kathy Kentopp wrote:

> The book challenged my beliefs and helped me clarify my role as a teacher. These things I learned will apply no matter where I teach. I had thought about teaching at a disadvantaged school, but shrugged it off because it seemed like a foreign country. For me a door may have opened to a life I could not conceive of before now.

Kathy also describes her experiences while reading *Small Victories:*

> I admire Jessica a lot, mostly because she is an idealist like me. She gave more than anyone expected of her. I easily identified. Soon instead of looking to see how to deal with unruly kids, I was reading to discover what caused underprivileged people. About halfway through I tried to focus on the positives as I always do in tough situations. The teacher's difficulties became mine, and I began to think about what I would do to survive. At the end, I refused to believe that Jessica would really leave

Figure 2.1. *Small Victories* one-pager by Bethany Lorence Natzke. (The text has been typeset from the original.)

QUOTATIONS—

"But at Seward Park, Jessica saw diseases more debilitating than sloth or deceit—an acceptance of inadequacy, a passive pitch into failure." (211)

"'So many of our kids,' he tells Ron afterward, 'don't even know when to capitalize.' That may be true, Ron replies, but many of his students lack the expressiveness and street wisdom and self-reliance of city children. They feel pressured to match their parents in status and income. They form their strongest bonds with their maids. They suffer socially for not having a car or the right car." (236)

"Angel cannot conceive of recycling as an environmental issue, only an economic one, and in his neighborhood nobody with any esteem would even consider the chore . . ." (239)

INTERPRETATIONS—

These chapters were again a bit discouraging. I came to see that my "bigger-than-life" Jessica was, in fact, human. She had her bad days just like everyone else. It did displease me greatly to see such a split in the comaradary [*sic*] of the teachers. I, at times, feared for Jessica's job because she often appeared to be the only one on her side. The only feeling that really explains my reactions is that I feel that her hands are tied. She doesn't have the materials or the support to really help her students learn and stay motivated. Everyone seemed to just want to get on with it at the department meeting, never letting Jessica, or anyone for that matter, speak their mind. If I were bound to certain rules and restrictions that dictated my teaching material and/or methods, I most certainly would feel at a loss . . . my plans would be in vain. I enjoyed the trip to the Friends Academy. Those poor little rich kids sure were ignorant!!! All their lives they have been spoon fed by their parents. They get the best of everything and never have to worry about a penny. Their lives are blissful and carefree. The Seward Park youths, on the other hand, have had to experience poverty and other such problems that come in an impoverished environment. They often go home from school only to go to work, and they need to work to help support their family. The rich are spoon fed . . . the impoverished must carve their way.

Figure 2.2. *Small Victories* one-pager by Jeff Smenyak.

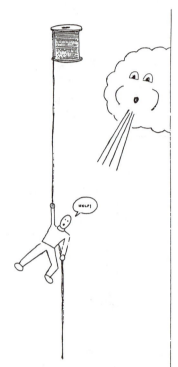

[teaching] until I read the very last page. I guess that's the difference between fiction and non-fiction.

My major purpose in choosing the book had been to raise for discussion issues of teaching and learning in the context of a culture different from the middle-class culture in which most of my students were raised and educated. The students discovered much more than I intended. They not only discussed issues, but they also experienced how it is to teach and learn in an urban high school through the eyes of Seward Park teachers and students.

For example, students experienced a variety of cultural attitudes and behaviors when they followed Dave, a truancy officer, into a New York City welfare hotel and when they read stories of recently immigrated students from Vietnam and Mexico. They realized the influence of students' cultures on their learning and classroom interactions, and they felt the frustration of students whose chances of getting an education were not only thwarted by their limited English, poor education, and poverty, but also by their teachers' lack of belief in them and the school district's disinterest in and unsupportiveness for their schools. They experienced the political and social forces that influence teachers' classroom behaviors and professional decisions as they watched Jessica in the teachers' workroom, with her journalism staff, in faculty meetings, and at the board of education. Their experiences far exceeded what I had hoped for and what students expected.

Another reason I chose to use *Small Victories* was to show students the benefits of using literature in a content class. One of these benefits is that through identification with the book's characters, readers come close to experiencing the events personally. As a result, they gain understanding as well as knowledge. The depth of these students' own identification with Jessica Siegel was a convincing example of this. They saw how tirelessly she worked to convince her students to expend the enormous effort required to go to college so that they could escape poverty and the prospect of meaningless lives. The students quickly realized that Jessica was an effective teacher because she valued her students and cared deeply for them. They began to see that student–teacher interaction is at the heart of teaching and learning and that dedicated teachers like Jessica measure their success by the quality and results of this interaction.

Many students were disappointed that even though several of her students won scholarships and gained college entrance, Jessica left teaching. Some believed she brought about her own burnout by caring too much. Some even said that one thing they learned from Jessica was that you need a life outside of school. Most students, however, were disappointed that there were so many obstacles placed in the way of dedicated teachers by the very groups that they expected would value and support dedicated teachers: other teachers, administrators, school districts, and parents.

Students were able to gain this broad range of experiences and insights because the response-centered relationships and practices of this teacher education classroom allowed and encouraged them to transact with the text—to make connections between their own educational experiences and beliefs and these new experiences presented in the book.

I couldn't help but relish the depth and liveliness of the discussions. We were talking about significant educational issues in real contexts. How to grade and what constitutes a good lesson are far more complex issues when considered in the context of school and when whole lives of students and teachers are involved. But there was still that nagging question: Have students learned the planned course content?

Kim Eastlund's response was encouraging:

> I think that I have learned more from our discussion on *Small Victories* than I have in any other education class. Although *Small Victories* is not a textbook, all of the important questions and issues are there. It addresses so many issues that I have never discussed before in a methods class. . . . *Small Victories* has forced me to seriously think about many things. I feel now that when I start my teaching, having come to conclusions on my values, objectives, etc., for the classroom, I will be better prepared to deal with a variety of situations. . . . I am really amazed how easily Jessica can draw students into her lessons by relating what they are going to discuss to the students' personal lives. I want to be able to do that too. Unfortunately, I fear that it is a lot harder than it appears in the book. I want to gain more confidence so that I do not feel limited to the typical "lecture and take notes" history class structure.

ASSESSING RESPONSE-CENTERED LEARNING

When I first began to use response-centered teaching practices in teacher education classrooms, my biggest challenge was to find ways to activate students' current knowledge and beliefs about particular content issues and then to plan experiences that would challenge them to reflect on new ideas and issues. While this will always be a challenge, I now see finding ways to evaluate students' learning as an even greater challenge. The "have they learned specific facts and information" dilemma raises its ugly head again.

Then there are the persistent questions about testing and grading. If I want to give students the "right" messages about learning, I have to trust that what they have learned is significant. If I fall back on traditional objective testing of facts and information, I give students the message that learning facts and information is more important than making connections and applying knowledge. I want to give them the opposite message. I also want to give students the message that they are the learners and that what they learn is dependent on their self-directed, and group-aided, learning process. Therefore, I need to ask them to tell me what *they* have learned.

I have developed an essay test, which I give at the conclusion of the first part of this course, that I believe gives these messages. I ask students to reflect on the ideas presented in the readings, including *Small Victories,* the class discussions, and their own experiences as teachers and learners and to describe their emerging philosophies of secondary school teaching. I ask them to address the student–teacher relationship, the teacher's and the student's role in learning, and to think about how their beliefs apply to their specific discipline.

Instead of a final test, I assign a final project in which I ask students to create a unit for a minimum of 5 days and then to write a paper in which they discuss the rationale for their choices of materials and methodologies.

This final project, the portfolio of one-pagers with its reflective paper, and the essay test replace more traditional types of evaluation in which the teacher asks questions and has specific answers in mind. These three nontraditional assessments require students to make connections between the new ideas and their current knowledge, beliefs, and experiences; to think about their theorizing as it applies specifically in their discipline; and to do something—describe their philosophy and plan a unit. As students demonstrate their growth in their own terms, their individual learning is validated. Evaluations of student learning, such as this, that value individual learning and response match other response-centered teaching practices.

Student course evaluations indicate that learning in a response-centered classroom helps students to enlarge and extend their philosophies of teaching and learning. A student wrote: "I have been forced to evaluate my own philosophy of teaching and have grown to understand both it and the concepts it is based on." Another student wrote:

> I learned the value of taking an interactive approach to learning. We must think about our own thinking and learning and expand on them as we work to expand our students' theories of the world (Smith [1985]). Learning is a collaborative process between teachers, students, and other students.

A third student wrote: "It helped me focus my theory of how students learn, and it made me realize the absolute need for relevance in the classroom."

Several comments indicated students were adopting a more critical approach to their practices. One student wrote: "I have learned to look at things more carefully—more critically—I have learned to be an individual as well as to work well with others in a group." Another student said: "I never asked why before this. I just accepted everything. Now I question myself and everything else." A third student attested to the type of learning that was occurring: "We were constantly thinking—not memorizing and regurgitating information. I learned a lot from others and about myself."

What these students have learned is certainly significant. In addition, their comments indicate that response-centered practices in teacher education classrooms open the spaces and encourage the thinking and reflection necessary to help beginning teachers build a philosophy of education based on response-centered assumptions. I plan to continue to model these practices so that future preservice teachers will experience this new way of learning and teaching and will acquire strategies and practices to use with their own students.

Are there any more questions? I certainly hope so. As long as questions continue to grow out of my teaching and theorizing, I know I am professionally alive. That is a good sign.

LITERATURE SELECTIONS

Clark, Johnnie. (1984). *Guns up!* New York: Ballantine.

Fa-yen, Wu-tsu. (1989). Zen and the art of burglary. In M. Stubbs & S. Barnet (Eds.), *The Little Brown reader* (5th ed.; pp. 342–343). Glenview, IL: Scott, Foresman.

Freedman, Samuel G. (1990). *Small victories: The real world of a teacher, her students & their high school.* New York: Harper & Row.

Lee, Harper. (1960). *To kill a mockingbird* (pp. 20–23). New York: Popular Library.

CHAPTER 3

I Still Have Not Stopped Asking, "How Can It Be Better?"

JOYCE WALLMAN

"How does a person come to acquire a love for literature?" This opening question in *Voices of Readers: How We Come to Love Books* by G. Robert Carlsen and Anne Sherrill (1988) has haunted me since I first encountered it. There is a general assumption that English teachers love literature, and indeed that is most likely true. Most English teachers arrive in the classroom first because they love literature, and second for the altruistic reasons for teaching. The slim text *Voices of Readers* was filled with quotes by readers of all ages. Surges of nostalgic memories rushed at me as I savored words that could have been my own. The richest gift my students might receive would be the love of literature and the desire to be lifelong readers; but it is not a gift given easily.

For years I have had an underlying unrest about the teaching of literature. It has seemed artificial and unnatural at times. Does the technical dissection of a text promote appreciation of that text or provide the skills to enjoy further reading? Do the questions at the end of the selection encourage genuine learning? What do "real readers" do when they read books? Reading is both a solitary and a social activity; shouldn't literature be shared? The word *sharing* has always had a pleasant connotation to me, but in the context of a classroom situation in which the teacher is asking students questions about their literature assignment, the sharing isn't always so pleasant. Furthermore, the questions aren't "real" because the teacher already knows the answers! How might I set up my classroom or teaching situation to encourage my students to love or least enjoy reading? And if they didn't enjoy reading a specific selection, how could they at least have a worthwhile encounter with the literature?

My concerns about fostering appreciation for literature stem from my own experiences in high school. Although I have very specific memories of examining the "metamorphosis" of Silas Marner, and watching Lady Macbeth deteriorate before my eyes, my fondest memories of high school English class are the Fridays on which our teacher would regularly let us read the books of our choice. Yes, as I remember, we paid our dues by turning in an essay first, and perhaps having a vocabulary test also, but for me, the reading time was a tremendous bonus. During the summer months I would make at least two trips a week to the library and eagerly gather a fresh supply of books; but from September to May my life was packed with other activities. I can still remember going to English class with the anticipation of escaping to Russia for 45 minutes through *Dr. Zhivago.* Now, with the wisdom of 17 years of teaching, I wonder if Mrs. Sisler could have taken grief for a "lazy" Friday or an "easy" lesson plan by allowing us to "just" read? Or could she have been so wise, even back in the 1960s? Perhaps she knew when to step back and allow us to help ourselves to the feast of literature.

How could I set up a situation in which my students could be real readers and become engaged with a piece of literature, not simply endure an assignment? I was frustrated with the tension, pressure, and anticipation of "Would this be a good day for class discussion?" Now and then there would be those magical moments (or are they "teachable moments"?) when the class would be lively and full of comments, disagreements, and insights; but most often you couldn't count on that. If my students were to be making strides in learning, why was I doing so much of the work? I wanted to remove the burden of discussion from my shoulders and encourage them to become active participants, not passive recipients.

English teachers always hold out the idealistic goal that students will love literature for the education and richness it can bring to their lives. But, more important, we hope that our students will enjoy reading and acquire the independent skills to make literacy a positive force for them. How might I make that contribution to their lives?

My chapter is the story of a fairly traditional English teacher who is always asking "How can it be better?" Like many colleagues, I was educated with New Criticism theory, but I was not poured in concrete! The underlying feelings and misgivings I have had for years made me ripe for a different approach to literature.

INTRODUCTION TO THE RESPONSE-CENTERED APPROACH

My initial experience using the response-centered approach to literature occurred when my colleague, Barb Livdahl, moved to a college English teaching position and began to pursue her doctoral degree. We had cooperated in preparation for many senior English classes and shared a common philosophy. Research in her doctoral program inspired her to try some new ideas in approaching literature. As she explains in Chapter 2, since she no longer taught in a high school classroom, she wondered if I would be willing to collaborate in trying a different approach. I readily agreed.

At our first meeting to discuss the project, she presented me with the book *In the Middle* by Nancie Atwell (1987). As with thousands of other language arts teachers, that book marked a turning point in my thinking about teaching and learning. As I read, I kept thinking "Yes! That's it! That's how it should be!" As I added ideas from Rosenblatt (1978), Probst (1988), Purves (Purves et al., 1990), and others, I began to see students and literature in my classroom in a refreshing way.

Barb's invitation seemed like an ideal opportunity to take a risk with the support of a superb educator. We planned to work with two ninth-grade classes of advanced English students who usually helped make the best of most learning situations. I realize, in retrospect, that I could have started with a poem or short story, but Barb and I were ambitious and selected a 325-page autobiographical selection about the Vietnam War. What follows is the narrative account of the process that I first used to incorporate the response-centered approach in my classroom. It includes responses from students as well as my own assessment and reflection.

THE PROCESS OF INCORPORATING THE APPROACH

I selected the book *Guns Up!* by Johnnie Clark (1984), which is his personal account of a Marine gunner during the Vietnam War. Although the book is fairly long, it reads easily and is an engaging story with no questionable language. This is the process that I followed in designing the unit:

1. Establish goals and expected outcomes.
2. Establish potential activities during unit.
3. Select response suggestions.

4. Establish schedule/time table.
5. Establish grading criteria.
6. Complete study of book.
7. Conduct post-study survey of students.

In keeping with my style as a fairly traditional teacher, I was thorough and methodical in my planning. Since Barb would document the process for her doctoral thesis, we were both anxious to have as much involvement with the planning as possible. (For a complete description of the research, see Livdahl, 1993.)

Establishing Goals

To put it simply, Barb and I wanted to know if the students would learn as much using the response-centered approach as they would using a traditional approach to literature. I therefore established the goals, framing them as "anticipated outcomes" (see Figure 3.1). Those would be the outcomes that I would consider important after a student encountered this book. I needed to value the meaning that each student created as he or she read the book. I wondered if the students' ideas of what was important were on my list at all!

In time, I came to realize that I had other goals that I didn't originally list, such as the strengthening of skills in thinking, reading, writing, oral presenting, and cooperative learning. These additional goals were not formally assessed, but I feel confident that students made substantial gains toward them.

Barb and I did not team-teach in this experiment; I was in charge of all the teaching responsibilities, and she served as collaborative planner and observer/recorder. I felt fortunate to have an experienced teacher and doctoral candidate in my room, for she was able to see many things that I wasn't able to observe. For all my lofty goals, I still had to stand in the hall between classes, take roll, sign absentee slips, handle makeup work, and mediate the disagreement between Mike and Josh. She was privy to revealing preclass talk and took notes on the conversation of one small group while I discussed with another.

Projecting Activities

After determining the goals for our study of this book, I generated ideas for potential activities to reach those goals (see Figure 3.2). I

Figure 3.1. Anticipated Outcomes of *Guns Up!*

During our reading and discussion of this book, I anticipate that students will
1. Gain a more realistic view of war
2. Think of war/peace in less abstract terms
3. Gain a sense of the geography of Vietnam and the theatre of war
4. Become more aware of the conflicting values and attitudes of the Vietnam Era in regard to this war
5. Discuss reasons why this war was so unpopular
6. React to the interpersonal relationships developed in this book
7. Respond to the characters in the book
8. Discuss the lack of plot and its effect on the story
9. Discuss the humor used by the author
10. Be aware of, or begin to recognize common or universal attitudes about the nature of war and effect on the people touched by it
11. Become aware of the individual criteria by which they evaluate books

Figure 3.2. Potential Activities for *Guns Up!*

1. Prewriting on the cover of the book. Share prewriting in small groups, then briefly summarize small group discussion with large group
2. Respond to the reading of the book after each of the five assigned portions (Refer to suggestions on response handout)
3. Oral sharing in small and large group discussions
4. Set up learning centers related to aspects of the Vietnam war such as maps, history, culture of the Vietnamese people, biography, perhaps related fictional selections
5. Use of the library for audiovisual materials and additional research source
6. Visual representation prepared in small groups, then presented to class
7. Interview with an adult who can share their perspective of the Vietnam era
8. Speaker: Marine who served in Vietnam
9. Use of related fiction or nonfiction videos
10. Potential coordination with history class
11. Final test—Group: movie production
    Individual: essay test

tried to select activities to accommodate different learning styles and varying levels of ability. Although my trial run using the response-centered approach was with two advanced English classes, I already knew that we would have untracked classes the following year and our classrooms would include students with a wide range of learning disabilities and emotional problems.

Suggesting Responses

My next step was to offer response suggestions (see Figure 3.3). I tried to incorporate responses that seemed specifically appropriate for this text, as well as rather ordinary suggestions. The text *Teaching Literature Nine to Fourteen* by Michael Benton and Geoff Fox (1985) offered excellent suggestions. I also wanted the response options to be open-ended to permit reluctant students as well as gifted students to feel challenged and successful. Today many of these suggestions have become routine for the students, as they use them often during their study of literature. I encourage students to bring their own ideas, and they frequently delight in being unique or unusually creative.

Establishing a Schedule

My next task was to establish a schedule for our study. I divided the book into sections, then set deadlines for reading and responding to each section. I set aside time for small- and large-group discussions, art activities, a test, and a visit from a Marine in our community. Two and a half weeks were reserved for this literature study.

Grading

I had decided that grades would not be critical because I already had many grades on which to determine student progress; that aspect would be secondary. However, since I was working with two classes of advanced English students, I knew they would be concerned with the grades even if I didn't consider that primary. Throughout the year they had been very competitive and grade conscious, so I knew I needed to be prepared with some concrete guidelines before we began our reading.

During my preparation of the unit I had divided the book into five sections. I determined that I would require a response after each section for which they would receive 5 points if it were ready on

Figure 3.3. Response activities for *Guns Up!*

During our study of this book you are asked to respond to your reading in several ways.

Required:

1. Complete five journal entries. Three of the five responses are to be written (about one page in length).
2. Participate in small group discussion in a manner that gives evidence of your reading ("good faith participation").
3. Conduct an Interview—At the completion of the book, you are to select someone who was living at the time of the Vietnam War and interview him or her. This should be written in the form of your choice.
4. All work is due on this date: _____

Your responses will be evaluated by the following criteria:

1. Evidence of careful reading and thoughtful writing.
2. Originality and creativity
3. A variety of responses

In preparation of your responses, consider these suggestions:

1. Reading journal responses—Speculate about the development, judgments, comparisons with your own experiences; reflect on moments or themes from the book; comment on how the author is telling the story.
2. Long term anticipation—How do you think the book will end? What can be seen in relation to the futures of individual characters in the book? (This response should be completed before you reach the halfway mark.)
3. Doodles—These must relate to the text.
4. Character's quotations—Select quotations from the reading that capture the essence of a character. Comment on how/why you see this quote as revealing.
5. Quotations—Choose quotations from the selected reading that you feel contain special meaning for the author or for you. Perhaps you might select quotes that reveal the author's attitudes about important issues or universal ideas.
6. Maps—Draw a map of Vietnam during this period and designate the places that are mentioned in the book.
7. Impression notes—Write your impressions of another character or event in the book perhaps in a form suggested by the book itself (a letter written from/to someone back home, a military communique, a radio or television news report on the war).
8. Thumbnail sketches—Make sketches of characters, setting or incidents, to sharpen the "pictures in the head."
9. Diaries—Write extracts from different characters' diaries, which might include their guesses about what might happen, their plans, their opinions of other characters, as well as accounts and appraisals of things past.

continued

Figure 3.3. Response activities for *Guns Up!* (continued)

10. "Dear Author"—a letter to the author of the book (via the publisher) containing questions, expressions of enjoyment, or reservations.
11. Character response—Select one or more characters and respond in depth to their actions, words, image, and physical appearance. You may include questions raised in your mind (answered or unanswered) and speculation about that character and his or her relationships with other characters.
12. Movie Review/Comparison—Write a review of a movie about the Vietnam War, and compare your impressions with Clark's book.
13. Vietnam update—Explain and discuss a current issue in regard to Vietnam in light of what you have learned from reading this book or related information.

Guidelines for the Interview—Select an adult that can share with you some impressions or memories of the Vietnam Era and how events of the time affected them. (Most any adult that was alive during that period of time.) Prepare at least six questions prior to your discussion, but be prepared to pursue questions that lead to a productive exchange. You are responsible for making it a substantial interview. If you don't get an adequate response, try someone else.

In your written report, identify your subject, and what their situation was during the time of the Vietnam conflict. You may record this in the form of a narrative, summary, or dialogue. Choose the most effective medium, not the easiest. It would be appropriate to include your reaction to the discussion. You may want to speculate on why the person responded as he or she did.

time and indicated some effort on their part. Tom Romano (1987) refers to this active, honest work as "good-faith participation" (p. 126). I have adopted his terminology and found it meaningful to the students. I simply asked them to have their journals open at the beginning of class, then walked around and checked that they had responded in some way. I made only occasional comments (always positive). It is impossible not to react to some artistic responses! I consciously make an effort to never have a noticeable negative reaction to a student's minimal or zero effort.

Each response could potentially receive 5 additional points when their journal was turned in to be read carefully by me. This part of their evaluation was labeled the "quality" grade. The terms of the "quality" evaluation were carefully outlined before the unit was begun. We discussed the kinds of connections that readers make with literature and looked at some sample student responses on the overhead projector. I encouraged them to try a variety of responses, although I required two of the five to be written. I invited them to make one response extraordinary; this response would be more carefully prepared to reveal a significant connection they had made with the literature. The form of this response was their choice. I emphasized that a quality response was *not* a summary of the reading or literary criticism that was designed to coordinate with my opinions. In general, a thoughtful response of notable effort would receive more quality points. Originality and creativity would be recognized as well.

To encourage extraordinary responses, I brought a cart of related books (fiction and nonfiction) to the classroom, in addition to offering a complete list of books available from our school library. Students used these for geographical reference, research on specific topics, and leisure reading relating to the Vietnam War.

Another part of a student's grade would be points received for a group activity, usually an automatic 10 or 20 points for completing the activity; but they could receive more or less depending on individual contribution to the group. (That scenario would be exceptional, however.) A test grade would also be part of a student's evaluation.

In typical fashion, the students questioned me thoroughly about grading before each assignment, activity, or test. However, after the completion of each item, there were no questions about or students who came to check on their grades. Considering that my trial run was done with advanced students, this was a shock! These highly competitive students became involved in the activities and seemed satisfied with their accomplishments. Final grades on the first unit ranged from A to D, but there were no complaints. The students had responded with a wide variety of creativity in art and writing. Even though grading criteria were not always concrete, I found that students had a fairly realistic assessment of their effort. With subsequent use of the response-centered approach, that has continued to be my experience. There is a strong sense of self-satisfaction for the work accomplished, not just the grade received.

EVALUATION OF THE APPROACH

The final aspect was to evaluate the response-centered approach. Could the students create meaning, raise and explore significant issues, and take responsibility for their own learning? Our evaluation process included a student survey, but ongoing activities were even more significant indicators of success.

After the third day of our initial experiment, Barb and I reviewed the written responses and notes from the small- and large-group discussions. It became apparent that all of the anticipated outcomes had been reached. We had 7 days left of our 2-week unit! My students and I had independently valued similar meanings from the text, but I questioned whether my original goals were too minimal. How much more could they derive from their transaction with this book than I had originally thought? This evidence was surprising, but promising.

The journal entries were clear evidence of interaction with the text. Barb recorded:

> Students' journal writings continued to reveal an almost urgent drive for meaning. As they read, they created secondary worlds of the Vietnam War. They became insiders, and thus responders, to these created worlds. . . . Students became involved in the issues of the war period. They empathized deeply with the soldiers. (Livdahl, 1993, p. 195)

One student wrote:

> Before, the Vietnam War had always been shadowed in my mind. I could have rattled off hundreds of things that happened in the American Revolution, Civil War, Spanish–American War, WWI, WWII, etc; but about the Vietnam War, which occurred just few years before my birth, I knew virtually nothing. Now having read *Guns Up!* I feel almost as if I'd lived through it. (quoted in Livdahl, 1993, p. 199)

The worthiness of a class discussion is a very subjective assessment. In fact, I would suggest that an immediate assessment is often unfair; the teacher should step away and allow the situation to come into perspective over time. To be honest, the small- and large-group discussions continually tested my patience. I often felt the students were too far "off task." There were days that I would ask Barb, "Is this really working? Are they really learning something substantial?" As we would review each day's progress, we would alternately encourage one another by recalling promising signs that we had observed. Invariably, she would have overheard meaningful exchanges amidst what superficially didn't appear significant. Barb's notes reveal student comments about small-group work:

It let people know my ideas, and me theirs on the war.

We got a lot of things covered and had fun talking about things we were interested in and things we like about the book.

We got to discuss some of the foreshadowing and characters' feelings in greater detail.

Barb continued:

> We were amazed at the authority and control these ninth-graders took over these discussions and the way they shaped them to serve their personal explorations and meaning making. (Livdahl, 1993, p. 195)

I recall a student telling me, "I learned more in our small group from Shannon [a young woman in the class] than I did from this book or history class!" The students became bolder in offering their opinions and insights, and I became more impressed with their thoughtfulness. There were certainly days that brought "thumbs-up" from both of us.

One day the large-group discussion revolved around a particularly gruesome scene from the book. David began relating the book to a discussion he had had with his father a short time before:

> My dad [a doctor] was telling me that it really was as bad as in this book—maybe even worse. He was in the field dealing directly with the wounded when he came on a young man who had been hit in the stomach. His guts were all over the place but other than that he was fairly unmarked. He asked my dad how he was doing, and my dad told him pretty well. He just scooped up his innards and put them back into the cavity and bound his middle up tight.

The class was silent and spellbound. I had to blink the tears from my eyes—not only from the tragedy that he described, but because I saw the text becoming palpably alive to the students. This kind of sharing isn't easily prompted by a teacher's questions.

Another measure of the students' learning was the group activity that served as an evaluation at the conclusion of our study. Students were to imagine that they had bought the movie rights for *Guns Up!* They were to prepare a presentation of their plans for the movie in order to obtain the funding from a "mysterious heiress." They selected the groups in which they wished to work, and the criteria for the assignment and grades were explained (see Figure 3.4). They had two class periods in which to prepare and were free to use out-of-class time if they chose.

The first class period of group work reflected the personalities of the group. The socially active "achievers" cleverly jockeyed for leadership roles, then spiritedly organized their approach. A more reserved group of students quietly maneuvered out of leadership roles and took a more group-supportive stance to achieve their goals. They seriously divided their responsibilities and proceeded in an organized way.

Yet another group of five young men came together reluctantly and even had trouble sitting near one another. One or two stood, and another was up and down. It took a great deal of restraint for me to allow them to have total "control" over their test preparation. There was a great deal of laughter, some singing, and no apparent organization. Fortunately, my fellow planner was also there to observe the activity. She casually stayed in the vicinity of this group and proceeded to take notes on their "discussion." Her written observations put the activity of this group into perspective:

> From the outside, it appeared this group accomplished nothing. Following their conversation, however, I realized that while they were not addressing themselves in a disciplined way to the test activity, they were exploring the issues surrounding the war. Their presentation was not as polished as others, nor did they have any advertising posters or pie graphs or bar graphs about their advertising budgets, but they understood that war was "hopeless" and "inhumane," and they wanted their audience to understand that too, so "we can prevent another war." They planned to focus on the psychological aspects of the war to show how the soldiers felt. They wanted people to leave the theater thinking about "not just Johnnie, but about all soldiers." And they wanted their audience to realize that the Vietnamese were people too. (Livdahl, 1993, p. 198)

It seems clear that they had created significant meanings from the text. The conversations in both small and large groups, the response journals, and the student surveys confirmed our classroom observations: The students had experienced a meaningful encounter with this piece of literature. They had actively taken responsibility for learning from this text.

Figure 3.4. Final Test for *Guns Up!*

This is an unconventional test that I expect you to take seriously. I would also like you to have some fun with it. If you can "get into it," I think your ideas will flow and you will share equitably in its completion.

Activity Description: Imagine that you have bought the rights to make a movie from this book. You want to create a very special movie, but you have many aspects to consider. You have a very wealthy potential backer of this production, a mysterious heiress, Countess Wallman. You are scheduled to make a presentation of your plan to obtain funding from her. A reliable source has informed you that she will be looking for your ideas on the following:

1. What is the box office appeal of this movie?
2. What audience will be the target of this movie?
3. What style of movie would be appropriate? (How much violence, how graphic, any special effects?)
4. What will be the major thrust of the movie?
5. What major issues would you choose to emphasize?
6. It would be difficult to use everything in the book. What will you include/omit?
7. Which characters will you use, or not use and why? How will you portray minor characters?
8. Which stars will you select for the specific parts?
9. How will you advertise or market this film?
10. What type of film is your goal? (money-making blockbuster, humorous, academy award winner, fine art film, "message" film)
11. How will the moviegoer view the war after seeing your film?
12. What music might you choose for this film? Do you have specific musicians in mind?
13. Will you maintain the style of dialogue from the book or will extensive changes be made?
14. Is there a major female role? Is there a romance? How? Why?
15. How will you portray the American soldier or the Vietnamese soldier in general? (poor, ignorant, drug-using, courageous, well-prepared, self-sacrificing)

Criteria for Grading: You will put this presentation together in a group of your choice. The presentation will be oral and is not to exceed ten minutes. It is expected that all members of the group should contribute to the work and the oral presentation. You will be graded on:

1. The quality of your group work. (Time well used, sharing of ideas, respect for others, willingness to cooperate and compromise.)
2. The quality of the material presented. Does it reflect thoughtfulness in regard to the text? Is the presentation thorough? creative? innovative? an authentic reflection of the book? Does the presentation reflect an understanding of the issues and ideas raised in the book?
3. The quality of the oral presentation. (Use of audiovisual aids accepted.) Are you organized, clear, appealing, convincing?
4. Adherence to the time allowance.

REFLECTIONS ON THE RESPONSE-CENTERED APPROACH

I find that interaction with the text becomes the responsibility of the students when we use the response-centered approach. They are free to take their range of experience, however extensive or limited, and relate that knowledge to the new experience of the text. "Learning is more likely to occur if both the teacher and the students believe that they can shape their worlds and are not victims of forces beyond their control" (Kirby & Kuykendall, 1991, p. 50). Students activate their own process of learning and thinking, rather than waiting for me to present the jewels of absolute truth.

The response approach has become an integral part of my classroom, but I still have not stopped asking, "How can it be better?" I have specific concerns in areas where I hope to see improvement. One concern is the less-than-ideal cooperative effort (group work). There are many variables affecting the quality of the group's endeavors, so it is a complex issue to address. Each year the efforts of the groups seem to improve as more classes adopt the cooperative learning approach. The social aspect of adolescents' interaction in the classroom continues to impact learning in a very powerful way. A study by Philip Cusick, *Inside High School* (1973), documents those powerful influences that can enhance the learning environment or threaten those opportunities. Judith Langer (1992) believes that teachers should develop classroom principles whereby students are

> supported to become socialized to engage in the process of literary understanding, exploring, rethinking, explaining, and defining their own understandings. The social structure of such classrooms calls for (and expects) the thoughtful participation of all students, and provides them with the environments in which they can see, learn, and practice these expected behaviors. (p. 51)

Another concern is the desire to encourage more meaningful writing. Students are reminded to make personal connections with the text and write to reveal engagement and serious intentions. I stress the freedom of writing with our own "voice." One student shared this frank observation: "It's hard to use your own voice when you don't feel comfortable with the reader." This was a sharp reminder to respect serious intentions. English teachers have nearly worn out the word *specific*, but detailed, introspective writing is essential to becoming an active learner. As students make connections with their experiences, background knowledge, and the literature, they begin to see the relevance of learning.

There have been many rewards for students as well as for me in the response-centered classroom. There is a much higher percentage of "on-task behavior." Recently, as we studied *Black Like Me* by John Griffin (1960), I charted classroom activity over the period of a week and a half. All but 1 to 10% of the students were seriously reading, writing, drawing, or discussing. I find that the best results occur when the students have a choice in their selection of literature. When possible, I try to offer several novels or short stories from which to choose.

Another factor about the response-centered approach that encourages the students to more honestly transact with the literature is that they are not under pressure to "like" the selection or even respond positively. Negative reactions are legitimate; however, students are expected to provide support for their responses. The result of this freedom is that there is more "genuine" reading, and less "faking" it. Cliff's opinion is no more significant than their own!

There is also a growth in the students' independent learning skills in approaching literature. No one tells them what to think, so they have to think for themselves. They have to read and formulate meaning within the framework of their prior experience and offer their own written, verbal, or visual response. There are not predetermined answers to the five questions at the end of the story or the study guide on the novel. Students can't just wait for a more verbal student to give the right answer; each student must have his or her own ideas about some aspects of the text. A "yes" or a "no" doesn't fit. The goal is that students will become autonomous readers.

In interviews with students, the overwhelming comment of students about literature class is the fear of giving a wrong answer in class and feeling "put down" or foolish. Even the brightest students continually use the word *intimidation* in regard to discussions about literature. A response-centered classroom promotes a positive atmosphere where critical reading and thinking skills can flourish.

In my experience, there is less emphasis on grades. Students feel more successful because the meaning that they construct from their reading is respected. They see themselves as capable learners who have control over their learning. If they choose not to respond to the literature, they don't receive the points. If they do a half-hearted response, they receive fewer points for their quality grade. When response writing is initially introduced, it is helpful for the teacher to offer a model response of her own. In order to provide additional models, I save student responses from previous years and share them from time to time; this reminds peers of the variety of writing styles and diverse viewpoints that are possible. When a more extensive unit involving responses is undertaken, I try to clarify specific criteria for grading before we begin. This seems to set the stage for more success and fewer misunderstandings.

Another positive aspect of the response-centered approach is that more students of varying abilities can be challenged to do their best. There are opportunities not only for verbal expression but for dramatic, musical, and artistic responses as well (see Figure 3.5). When they are especially artistic, I have enjoyed watching some healthily competitive "one-upsmanship." There are always markers, scissors, glue, and paper available in the room for individual responses or group work. When their reading portion is complete, students can go to the library for additional research. The artistic opportunities (visual, dramatic, and musical) have been most rewarding for me as a teacher. I have seen so many distinctive interpretations of the literature. Character depictions have created fresh visions. Students often capture specific scenes that slip by other readers.

Visuals also provide opportunity for depicting symbolism without any prompting from me. I recall specifically a group of students who spent two class periods protectively huddled over their poster consisting entirely of symbolic items, arrangements and colors to represent the major meanings of an entire book. When they presented their product to the class on the third day, their self-satisfaction soared as the class spontaneously applauded their work. A question from the teacher regarding symbolism in literature can chill the room in a hurry, but when it is the students' idea, it is a different story.

Using the response-centered approach isn't a lesson plan to try one day. It is a part of a philosophy of learning, thinking, and making meaning. It involves the teacher's releasing control as dispenser of knowledge and giving responsibility for learning back to the students. It is establishing a classroom environment that enables students to take risks. It is establishing a relationship among learners who value the process and respect the effort of those who participate. The classroom must be free from intimidation, a safe place to take risks.

It involves a new way of asking questions and prompting students. Robert Probst suggests, "Questions that focus upon readers, rather than upon texts, are appropriate" (quoted in Langer, 1992, p. 67). It involves new ways of listening and responding to students. A

Figure 3.5. Visual Representation of Literature

Your assignment today is to prepare a visual representation of the book that your group read. You are to draw scenes, people, objects, symbolic items or images that represent your most vivid impressions from the book. You may organize the project in the way that your whole group finds most appealing. You may fairly divide responsibilities or share in the whole production.

The intent of this activity is to share viewpoints on the book and bring some key ideas or issues into better focus. You will not be judged on your artistic talent.

Today's work is worth 10 points.

Grading criteria include:
1. Cooperation/contribution/compromise within your group (leadership appreciated also)
2. Use of time—being productive and on task (includes not bothering others)
3. The quality of your product
   - creativity of thought
   - creativity of product
   - originality
   - authentic reflection of the book
   - representation of important issues relating to the text

You will have this class period only.

Be prepared to present your representation to the class tomorrow. You should be able to explain your product to the class within the context of the entire book.

response-centered classroom is response in many ways. It is not telling a student he or she is wrong and has misinterpreted the literature. It is examining the process by which a student has constructed meaning and recognizing the divergent paths to arrive at meanings. It is sharing meanings and being flexible to other viewpoints, and being able to change your own.

As I continue to read research about response and incorporate it into my classroom, I realize how much I have to learn. The way I formulated the process 4 years ago has changed, and what I do next month will undoubtedly change as well. The response-centered approach is the foundation for encounters with literature in my classroom; however, I still feel comfortable approaching some especially challenging literature with more traditional methods. The response-centered approach seems most rewarding with highly engaging, "age-relevant" literature.

Creating a response-centered classroom is an ongoing process. This approach has become part of a growing philosophy in my teaching about how I view students and learning. The needs of the class, individual student, and teacher are always in flux. Classes tend to take on a collective personality, and part of the responding needs to be in reaction to that as well. The available literature and support changes, and that becomes a factor also.

I described myself as the voice of a traditional teacher looking for ways to reach students through methods that would foster life-long learning skills and patterns. I often feel like a teacher in the middle—not willing to disregard past successful methods and experiences, but recognizing that new approaches are worth examining. I am constantly reminded that learning is a very complex process with countless variables.

The response-centered approach has offered promising results in my classroom, but I still ask myself every day, "How can it be better?" Recently, I completed Linda Rief's book, *Seeking Diversity* (1992). Her ideas and spirit have prompted significant changes in my classroom this fall, but she offers a realistic reminder:

> I am not Nancie Atwell or Tom Romano, and I can never do exactly what they do in the same way they do it. We all carry our own personalities, histories, and agendas into a room the minute we step in. I adapted and changed their ideas, their structures, their strategies to fit me and my kids. What I do today, I may not do tomorrow. One thing will remain constant: I will always have questions. (p. 4)

My classroom is also unique to my personality and the background that I bring to it, but like other concerned teachers, I will always have questions.

LITERATURE SELECTIONS

Clark, Johnnie. (1984). *Guns up!* New York: Ballantine.
Griffin, John Howard. (1960). *Black like me.* New York: Penguin.

CHAPTER 4

Inviting and Respecting
Real Response

TERESA KRINKE HERBERT

BEGINNING QUESTIONS

Throughout these past 3 years, I have come to understand my crucially important role in enabling the adolescents who fill my classroom to feel respected and trusted. These young people have taught me that their voices must be heard and acknowledged or else, in their own way, they will excuse themselves early from the table of learning.

I had sensed this to be important when taking my preservice education courses. During this time I envisioned my ideal classroom as a place filled with excitement: students and teacher excited about working with relevant topics and activities, and a place where people were content to be. Visionaries such as Nancie Atwell (1987) inspired and certainly prompted me to redefine my own beliefs about how people learn. Yet, unfortunately, many of my ideas were also born out of frustration I had experienced as a student in past language arts classrooms. I can still clearly recall staring painfully at a multiple-choice literature test, wavering between the frustration of trying to decode the "trick" question I knew had to be there, and feelings of failure because I did not read *Tom Sawyer* the way I obviously should have.

During our first summer retreat as a collaborative group, it became even more apparent to me that such frustration was unnecessary and that I wanted to do whatever I could to ensure that future students in my classroom would not have to experience such frustration or sense of failure. Our reading and discussions about response-centered curriculum both inspired and challenged me to find alternative methods in teaching literature unlike the too-familiar traditional methods I experienced as a student.

As I write this chapter, now 3 years after our first collaborative meeting, I must admit that I do not claim to be a "response" expert. I am as much, or more, a student today as I was 3 years ago, except that I have learned much since then about adolescents and reading and writing processes. Each day that I try different response approaches in my classroom, I learn something new. I am learning even as I write this chapter, because learning, like reading and writing, is a process.

The beliefs behind response theory which we discussed that summer—that students' voices were allowed in the interpretation of a text, and that students' ideas, not so much the teacher's, were central to the curriculum—sounded extremely liberating. I was excited about the possibilities of a classroom where students would have choices in what they read, would be asked to share their knowledge and experiences through a variety of means, and would be challenged to think critically. My goals at that time were similar to Purves's statement about a response-centered curriculum:

> The aim of the curriculum is to affect students' perceptions of works of art (literary works), to improve their ability to articulate their responses, to increase their tolerance of the diversity of human responses to similar objects, and to bring them together into a community of communities. (Purves et al., 1990, p. 57)

Thinking of a new model of teaching was equally as challenging as it was exciting. This type of approach, I thought, had to work, but I struggled greatly with its practical application. How would this look in practice? What about evaluation? And how could I prove that this approach might possess both integrity and greater reward for both student and teacher?

Student Teaching

From our first session together, I clung to this question, which guided my lesson planning that fall during my student teaching: How can I tap into each student's "theory of the world?" (Smith, 1985, p. 73). I wanted the structure of my lessons to be filled with many openings in which students could fit their ways of thinking and interpreting a text. Some of these openings, or means of sharing one's responses, I envisioned as being written, artistic, or dramatic in form. This question, however, led me to experiment with what I now consider some rather silly and even contrived methods of seeking out our ninth-graders' theories of the world.

Being somewhat limited to following the established ninth-grade curriculum and textbook, Joyce, my cooperating teacher, and I decided to try putting this theory into practice by creating a short story unit using stories from the class textbook. With Joyce's help, I selected five stories and decided to connect them with the theme "choices." Our basic intention was to use this theme not exclusively but as a common strand with which we would ask the students to compare all the stories.

My guiding question contained value in that it reminded me to keep our students central to my lesson planning; however, I was somewhat led astray in thinking I had to aid students in bringing their world theories to surface *prior* to reading each story in our unit. Such thinking seems now to imply that I did not sufficiently trust my students to naturally apply their unique thoughts, questions, and perceptions during the reading process. Trusting the students to be independent thinkers and learners was one of my strongest beliefs, yet I inadvertently failed to do this in some of my planning.

The unit began by having the students do a word reflection (as described in Chapter 1) on the word *choices.* I asked the students to write down the images, words, phrases, or ideas that came to mind when thinking of the word *choices.* All of us in the class shared our individual reflections. Students' reflections included words that alluded to choices they often make, such as choices about friendships, sports, and future plans; the morning choices they must make; and choices in watching television. Many also used words that described the impact of choices—words such as *life-changing, good and bad, pressure,* and *force.* Later they gathered in small groups to share their reflections with others. I asked them as a group to somehow categorize their collective group choices, a task requiring them to compare their various lists and identify both common and unique ideas. Each small group then shared with the whole class their list of categories. This activity proved to be useful in that each student was able to have a voice in describing the implications of choices in their lives. Also, since each student was an experienced choice-maker, each could be included in the reflection and discussion.

Our discussions about choices continued throughout our reading of the various short stories. With each story we spent some time analyzing the choices made by the characters in the story. For example, "The Lady, or the Tiger?" by Frank Stockton (1980) tells of a semibarbaric king whose daughter had a secret love affair with a common man whom the king found unsuitable. Once the king discovered the relationship, he forced his daughter's lover to face his random justice system using two doors. Behind one of the doors the king had placed a very fierce tiger, and behind the other a damsel of the court who invoked great feelings of jealousy in the princess. Being present at the "trial," the princess makes a discreet motion toward one of the doors. This gesture is witnessed by her lover. Readers of the story are left to speculate about the decisions of the princess and the young man: Would the princess desire her lover to be married to another woman of whom she did not approve, or that he be eaten by the tiger? And would her lover trust her and open the door to which she signaled, or open the other door?

After students had read this story, we asked them to define, using their own knowledge and language, the terms *fate, chance,* and *choice.* We then asked them to share their definitions with their small groups of four to six members. After sharing they were to pull their knowledge together from all members of the group to create a definition for each of the three words. Next, they were to decide, as a group, which of these words or concepts had the greatest impact in the story and which had the least. Eventually, they were to come to a group consensus in ranking the words, number 1 being the most important, to number 3 being the least. They were to share with the whole class their group rationale for their ranking order.

The resulting discussions were lively, as students negotiated the definitions of these three closely related terms, and also as they tried to sort out the events of the story that were significantly affected by either fate, choice, or chance. The students were not being asked to find the one right answer (my interpretation of the story), but rather were asked to share their own interpretations and examples from the story that would support those ideas.

This was one class discussion where I felt that students were really investing their energies as they struggled to define concepts that were not completely familiar to everyone in the group. They naturally discussed important elements in the story such as the irony in the ending, where the young man was doomed with either of his door choices. They argued about whether or not the man would trust the princess, his lover, and open the door she indicated for him to open. Some felt certain she would not betray her lover, and others challenged their group members to consider the opposite.

At the time, this activity felt very successful because of the lively interaction between students and because it seemed like each student was able to have an active voice in the interpretation of the text. However, 3 years later, I have to stop and wonder if this type of an activity is still too controlling of the text's interpretation.

There seems to be a very thin line between guiding students to deeper interpretations of a text, and yet ensuring that students are independent, critical thinkers, not people dependent on a teacher to guide them through a literature discussion. In this assignment, I had hoped that our ninth-graders would use their own interpretations of the text, share those with other classmates, and challenge their own and others' understanding of the story by looking at the story through the broader scope of the three concepts we selected.

As I reflect now, though, this process seems perhaps to contain many of the same qualities as a traditional, teacher-driven literature lesson. The concepts of fate, chance, and choice were all selected by the teacher, not the students. Although students were asked to share with the group their definitions and applications of those definitions to the story, I wonder if we heard true voices rather than the standard "follow the directions, please the teacher" voices. A combination might have occurred; however, I did feel like I had given my students a better chance than if I had asked them to complete the discussion questions at the end of the story. I can only hope that our class discussion was more stimulating than having to write responses to such questions as: "From what you know of the princess, which do you think she would point to: the lady or the tiger?" (Stockton, 1980, p. 23).

My intention to allow students to share their world theories was evident in a rather odd lesson plan for another story we read, "The Balek Scales" by Heinrich Boll (1980). This is a story about the injustice a young boy and some village members experienced with an inaccurate scale used to weigh the goods that the townspeople were selling. In my student teaching journal for that day, I had written at the day's end: "I wanted to create a situation similar to the situation which Franz Bucher, the main character in the story, experienced. I wanted to use something which would be important to them so they could truly sense some kind of injustice and would care enough to speak out against it. I decided upon grades."

Prior to reading the story, I told the students that I had developed a new, point-based grading system. A scale was used to weigh only six students' writing utensils, and points were given based on the mass of those utensils. Only one-fifth of the class had the opportunity to receive points that day. The others were told that perhaps some other day they would get their chance.

We took a vote later during the class period on whether to keep the new system or to drop it. All classes, not surprisingly, voted for the latter. In the end, there were students who did believe me and were upset at the system; students who didn't believe me and were waiting for the game to end; and many students who were quite confused as to what their student teacher was up to.

Although my intentions were honest in that I wanted to help our students call to the front of their minds that which they already knew about justice, the situation I had created was not real, and so I don't think that I helped them understand "The Balek Scales" any differently than if I had not done this silly role-play. I did, perhaps, entertain or raise their curiosity in reading the story, but how much I aided their comprehension and responding to the story is debatable.

Adolescents certainly have pre-established ideas about the concepts of justice and injustice. Perhaps I could have trusted the students to compare their own experiences of justice and injustice, rather than trying to place them in a fictitious replication of the story and then asking them to respond. Everyone has stories to tell of times they've experienced unfair treatment. I'm afraid that the activities I did with our ninth-graders were too controlling. If we provide quality literature (a problem when limited to an older textbook) and allow students to respond from their authentic voices (not necessarily answering the teacher's questions), then we are doing more to help students respond authentically. What I did, I hate to admit, was use a rather inauthentic method to aid students' responses. I share this grief as described by Mem Fox (1993): "I realized with grief that purposeless activities in language arts are probably the burial grounds of language development and that coffins can be found in most classrooms, including mine" (p. 6).

During those 10 weeks of student teaching, my assumption that teaching was truly a rigorous and exciting profession became a reality. Working with Joyce and others in our group provided me great encouragement to take risks in trying new methods and also offered me listening ears, experienced guidance, and perspectives I viewed with high regard. I appreciated the opportunity, in a preservice setting, to refine a nontested philosophy, a philosophy based primarily on my experiences in student, not teacher, shoes. Once I stepped into those teacher shoes, I could begin testing my/our philosophy of how adolescents could best learn with literature.

Having the opportunity to work with my cooperating teacher prior to the start of my student teaching was invaluable for me. I was really able to get to know and develop a positive working relationship with Joyce before my student teaching assignment began. Early on we discovered our similarities and differences, and knew what to expect from each other. This, I knew, was unique for a student teaching experience. I felt great security beginning the school year knowing that we had already established a positive working relationship after having had the opportunity to share our own personal beliefs and experiences in education, and more than that, had struggled together to define what we as a group of teachers envisioned a response-centered classroom to be. I felt safe in taking risks in Joyce's classroom, which I knew could not be said for all student teaching environments.

First-Year Teaching

My first teaching job, the succeeding year, brought me to another junior high school and, fortunately, a group of risk-taking, student-centered English teachers who had already been enveloping themselves and their students in process writing, using a writing/reading workshop approach. For the past 5 years they had been experimenting with allowing their students a voice in selecting writing topics and books to read. I was very fortunate to join this dedicated group of professionals. My ambitions to continue exploring methods of response-centered teaching were fully supported by them, since they, too, were seeking to teach literature with methods more closely patterned to their beliefs about how adolescents learn language. I quickly realized that I had walked into a very unique setting of teachers who paralleled me in my developing philosophy.

For the first part of the year, I wanted to try a reading/writing workshop approach similar to what my colleagues were using, so I began the year by inviting my students to select their own writing topics and books that they wanted to read.

In order to find out what my students were thinking about their reading, I borrowed a "book report" format developed by one of my colleagues. These reports were to be completed at least twice a week in the students' writing notebooks and could be done at any point in their reading, not just at the end of the book.

In these informal book reports the students were to do four things, the first being to give *compliments* to the author on what they enjoyed or thought had been done well in the writing. The second was to offer their *criticism* of what did not work for them as a reader, or what they thought could have been written differently or more effectively. Next they were to share *questions* about the text that arose for them as they read. Lastly, they were to *compare* the text to other pieces of writing and/or to memories from their own lives of which the book reminded them.

I liked the structure of this book report for a couple of reasons. First of all, since students were reading a wide variety of books, from Maya Angelou to L. M. Montgomery and Christopher Pike, and were at different places in each of these books, it was difficult to create an assignment that required students to think critically, yet not be stifled. This report could also work for all the various genres my students were reading.

My seventh- and eighth-graders really enjoyed and seemed to respect the freedom to choose their own books and the long periods of time that were given in class for silent reading. However, their response to doing the book reports was not overwhelmingly positive. Perhaps just the fact that it was an assignment turned some off, but I think in choosing to call the assignment "book reports" we invited in all their past knowledge and impressions of book reports from former language arts classrooms. Even though I verbally acknowledged that my directions might be unique, many students were unable to look beyond the title.

The responses that they gave in these reports varied. Some would invest deep thinking in interpreting the text, offering lengthy, thoughtful compliments, questions, criticisms, or comparisons. Others slugged along, possibly covering each of the required areas by quickly filling the pages with less than thoughtful sentences such as "It was good" or "It was stupid."

Much time was spent in trying to model more thoughtful responses, responses that would show rather than tell an opinion. Yet if students really could not find a reason to care about the book report, then the subsequent writing continued to be limp and meaningless.

Even some students who wrote more thoughtful book reports expressed some resentment of the assignment. I gathered this from such comments as: "These are boring!" or "Do we have to do book reports?" or "Can't we just read?" My initial response was to cringe with discouragement. The next temptation was to brush off such comments, attributing them to lazy attitudes. But then I began to wonder, really, what message they were sending me in saying that this assignment was not enjoyable. Were they saying that it was challenging? That they could not understand the relevance to their lives? That it was too formulaic? Or were they just letting me know that they had had it up to here with book reports? Student laziness can too easily become a teacher's excuse for not taking a more careful look at why a particular method is ineffective. My search for alternative response options continued.

Second-Year Teaching

In my second year of teaching, I changed this weekly literature response to another form, the "one-pager," a format I borrowed from Barb. She had used one-pagers with students in her education courses (see Chapter 2). In my classes, the one-pager became a "two-pager" since my students were used to skipping lines for revision purposes in their writing notebooks. I asked them to respond twice a week to their reading, wherever they were at, by including:

1. One visual representation of their reading.
2. One quotation from their reading.
3. Interpretive paragraphs that explain connections and questions developed from the story.

I found this approach to be much more successful than the book reports. Students were much more reflective, and many seemed actually to enjoy doing them. For the adolescents who enjoyed drawing and illustrating their writing, they were able to create some very thoughtful symbols in their responses.

Gina, an eighth-grader in one of my classes, had chosen to read *Ordinary People* by Judith Guest (1976). The book, she admitted, challenged her, yet in her visual representation and interpretive statement Gina showed that she definitely was able to understand many complex relationships in the story, and she beautifully symbolized those relationships by using a spider web metaphor (see Figure 4.1).

A more typical eighth-grade two-pager was done by Julie when reading *The Third Eye* by Lois Duncan (1984). This was one of Julie's first two-pagers. Her visual symbol was somewhat less complex than Gina's web metaphor, yet she made a significant connection between the description of a beautiful scene in the story and her great concern about the destruction of the earth's environment. This was a real connection between a written text and an eighth-grader's concern for the well-being of her planet. Julie realized that she had a role in preventing this destruction, and she was seeking to do what she could to preserve what is beautiful in life. This response, although not long, was definitely real and definitely significant (see Figure 4.2).

Figure 4.1. Gina's two-pager for *Ordinary People*. (The text has been typeset from the original.)

This picture represents the web of failure that Conrad Jarrett feels he is caught in. His brother, Jordan, died and so Conrad feels he has to now take his place. This causes him to commit suicide to punish himself for not being perfect. His parents and friends find it difficult to adjust to the absence of Jordan and the "new" or "different" Conrad.

"Cliches. They jump out at you from everywhere, but you never see your own." p. 29

"Christ is the Answer—What was the question?" p. 4

So far I've found that this book is kind of hard to follow. I've almost given up on it a couple of times, but I keep coming back to it! The way in which the author has written more about emotions and the characters' feelings rather than mostly actions intrigues me. There is a little too much swearing for my taste. As I've progressed in my reading I've wondered what happened to Jordan, his brother, and why Conrad doesn't get along with his mother. I just found a quote I like. Here it is: "Too much thinking can ruin you." I'm going to continue reading this book, so hopefully it will become clearer.

Figure 4.2. Julie's two-pager for *The Third Eye*. (The text has been typeset from the original.)

This flower represents a very beatiful [*sic*] place we live in.

"Then she registered that the sound had been a bird call. Opening her eyes, she found herself confronted with a scene that was unlike anything she could ever have imagined. She was lying in the midst of a dazzling fairy tale world composed of giant spires with sculptured bases, all glinting an impossible shade of salmon in the stinging brilliance of the glittering morning light. Behind these rocks that glowed a sky that was the same vivid incredible blue as Ron Wilson's eyes."

This paraghraph [*sic*] made me remember that we have a great and beautiful planet earth and that we should always charish [*sic*] it. We only have one earth and it needs to last forever. Right no it is being destroyed at a very fast rate. We need to think about what we do before we do things. Some people are not even aware of what they do. Earth is very important to everyone and we need to treat it correctly.

Literature's vast potential to awaken humans to that which is beautiful in life should not be undermined by teachers who require students to interpret literature in the way they perceive to be right. This, I fear, might have occurred had I required the students to take a multiple-choice test at the end of reading their novels.

RESHAPING QUESTIONS: STILL SEARCHING FOR REAL RESPONSE

About midway through the year, I became frustrated that for many of the students, doing two-pagers was still writing for the teacher, merely completing a class requirement. They were not writing to share with anyone else, just for me. That was very motivational for the students who truly cared about my response; however, I must admit that my response did not move some students to write thoughtful responses, much less write anything at all.

So my questions changed again. In the final quarter of the year, I told my students that instead of the two-pagers, we were going to try a different type of literature response until the end of the year. I explained my concern that some were writing only for me, and that I wanted this to be not just another assignment but writing that would have meaning and purpose for them. The students were still reading books they had chosen to read. I asked them to form a reading group of two to four people. These people, I told them, would be the ones with whom they would share their ideas about their books.

Since we were involved in process writing at the same time, I did not have time to give them any kind of written response to their two-pagers. I thought it was important that they share the meanings they had created in their reading with others because in doing so, other layers of meaning have the potential of being created. Also, their writing often takes on more significance if they understand their audience to be wider than the teacher alone. Perhaps if they were sharing these ideas with their peers, I thought, the writing would have a more authentic purpose for them.

The directions were rather simple—they were to write to their partner(s) at least every other day about their reading. I did not carefully outline what format to follow (other than that it be a letter), and I did not spell out the assigned content of their letters. What I suggested was that they exchange ideas similar to those they shared in their two-pagers—interpretive responses to their reading. They might want to share some summary of their book if their partner(s) were not familiar with the book, but I suggested that they go beyond that and show their group what they as readers thought about the events, characters, facts, or issues they discovered in their reading. Some decided to select a new book to read together as a group, while others continued reading their own individual books. Each week I tried to set aside at least one-half to one full class period where they could work with their partners, passing notebooks back and forth to each other and writing letters.

Their first few letters to each other were, for the most part, summary-type writing, yet they needed to begin somewhere. After a few weeks, though, I began noticing more exciting things happening in these letters, some of which I hadn't anticipated. The tone, content, and purpose of writing changed for many. They began to ask more questions of each other about their books—more how and why questions. Why did this character act in this way? How could such a thing really happen? I read many questions seeking to find out how a partner's story had progressed, and I read many "Your book sounds interesting or scary, I will have to try it" comments.

Connections were being made to one another as persons and as readers. I was very pleased that for many, this mattered. They could communicate with peers about their books in their own language. To my delight, some students were able to create connections between the different books they were reading. For example, Ellen was reading a book about ancient civilizations while Anne was deeply engrossed in *Jurassic Park* by Michael Crichton (1990). Their responses to one another were exciting as they connected the content of their books and also discovered shared interests and concerns along the way. They acknowledged their appreciation of one another in their letters: "You really know what triggers my thoughts," Ellen wrote to Anne, and Anne responded with, "I appreciate your comments too. It's fun to converse with someone who has as much insight on life as you." This to me shows real readers, real literature, and real connections being formed.

As I experiment with various methods of teaching and allowing students to respond to literature, I must reflect and refine. I have learned that in order to be fair to students and to new methods or new questions I ask, I must allow time—weeks, perhaps months, for all of us to adapt and grow. Students need not only great amounts of time to explore a new method, but they also need to see modeling by me. I would join various groups and write to a student about the books I was reading. When I read some of our comments that reflected significant connections and questions, I would often make a transparency so that I could share them with all the students. They need to see how responses might look when they reflect rich, multi-layered thinking—and also how they look when the thinking seems more shallow.

THE INEVITABLE QUESTION: HOW DO WE EVALUATE THIS LEARNING?

Teaching literature this way—with an emphasis on student responses and questions to a text—seems different than a more traditional method of teaching. My classroom is not always quiet, nor might it appear "controlled" like other, more traditional classrooms where everyone is reading the same piece of literature at the same time, or taking the same quiet test all at once. Certainly we do have days where everyone quietly reads or writes, but more often there are a variety of activities occurring simultaneously. "Messy" is one of my favorite ways to describe this way of teaching. I am the first to admit that when students are working in various groups and on different types of projects, knowing what each student is doing every second of the hour is impossible. I must be an active agent, weaving in and out between groups, inquiring and trying to help students identify and shape their responses. Being messy doesn't make me uncomfortable, as it once did, because it means that many different student voices are being acknowledged and explored. It seems different because it is different.

Although this type of teaching is different, I am still accountable to the traditional system of evaluation. At the trimester's end, I must darken in those holes that translate to an A, B, C, D, or F, and somehow I and my students must find a bridge that will connect the meaning of those letters with the learning that has occurred. I have attempted various evaluation approaches—everything from putting an individual number or letter grade on an individual or group visual collage, video, skit, or writing, to having groups of students determine other students' project grades. Quickly I discovered that evaluating in this manner of assigning grades to individual responses was less than successful. Students too easily became disconnected from their responses because our dialogue tended to center around those letters or numbers rather than their ideas and representations of those ideas.

I have started requiring students to take some of the responsibility in evaluating their own work, asking them to show me, either in writing or verbally, the parts of their responses that reflect deeper thinking. The means I use to solicit my students' thinking about their work changes, as do the students who enter my classroom each year. My search for accurate means of evaluating is ongoing. What works one year might not the next.

I realize this evaluation road we travel is made to appear straight, with clearly defined boundaries; but it is not. It can be quite bumpy, leading us through many perplexing bends and turns. What I have learned is that my students must remain connected to their work. Without their voices, their perceptions about the new knowledge they have created, I cannot know what understandings they have come to, or what learning has taken place. They need time to develop their responses, time to sift through what they have created, so that they can make decisions about the meaning and quality of their responses to the literature they read.

"Response" has come to encompass many, many different interpretations and applications in language arts textbooks and classrooms. I am still searching—not for the single, best approach, but rather for approaches that will invite the greatest potential of response for the hundreds of students who fill my classroom year after year. What works for one student might not for the next. What I do know, though, is that in order for successful learning to happen in my classroom, each student must feel respected as a competent reader, writer, learner, and human being. Respecting and trusting that my students are capable of making decisions about a written text is the place I must begin if I want to attempt a response-centered approach in teaching literature in my classroom. It is sometimes messy, but always worth it.

LITERATURE SELECTIONS

Boll, Heinrich. (1990). The Balek scales. In F. Safier (Ed.), *Adventures in reading* (pp. 132–139). New York: Harcourt Brace Jovanovich.
Crichton, Michael. (1990). *Jurassic Park*. New York: Ballantine.
Duncan, Lois. (1984). *The third eye*. New York: Little, Brown.
Guest, Judith. (1976). *Ordinary people*. New York: Viking Penguin.
Stockton, Frank. (1980). The lady, or the tiger? In F. Safier (Ed.), *Adventures in reading* (pp. 19–23). New York: Harcourt Brace Jovanovich.

CHAPTER 5

The Most Precious of All Mysteries

DEBRA KRAMER GEIGER

Above my desk at the middle school where I work, a small poster is tacked: a quotation from one of my former high school teachers. Tom Melchoir, a language arts teacher in Burnsville, Minnesota, was Minnesota Teacher of the Year in 1971. He said, "I teach because it is a noble profession and because it focuses on the most precious of all mysteries, the human spirit."

"I teach students, not English," I've heard people say. As obvious as it is, I have found that I have to keep reminding myself of that fact. I am engaged in a struggle to plan and teach a curriculum that will prepare students to operate as mature, literate members of our society, while respecting, above all else, the mystery and fragility of each of the young "spirits" I work with. It's so easy to let the curriculum come before the students. Outcomes and outlines and performance indicators can look so good on paper: so clean, clear, measurable, defendable. Under the scrutiny of the school board and the state department of education, it's easy to let the standardized test scores be the sole objective of instruction. But my intuition and my day-to-day experience tell me that students are not "standard"; they are individuals and have special needs that must be attended to, voices that must be heard, or they will opt out of the learning opportunities in my classroom.

I think this must be what is referred to as the "art" of teaching. I know it certainly can't be learned by reading the teacher's edition of the textbook, where "Differentiation of Curriculum for Special Needs Students" (aren't they all special needs students?) is addressed in a little blue box in a sidebar or at the end of the unit. And I know that others of my colleagues must be engaged in this struggle, too, because our staff is invited each year to be inserviced on topics such as "Differentiating the Curriculum," "Teaching the Gifted," and

"Addressing the Needs of Special Education Students in the Mainstream."

My work with our group of teacher-researchers has spanned the entire length of my teaching career; more and more, I'm realizing that these people (Teresa, Janice, Joyce, Barb, and Karla), the conversations we've had, and our collective experiences in response-centered classrooms have been the most powerful force in shaping my understanding of my role as a teacher. I think the most valuable thing I have gained from this experience is confidence in my ability to go "back to the basics" of what I believe about learning: My students come to the classroom with already well-formed and fairly sophisticated working "theories of the world" (Smith, 1985), and learning takes place—knowledge is created—when students interact with a new idea or concept or piece of literature, and their views of the world are stretched. The more I can focus on the essential nature of what goes on in the learning arena, the less I have to worry about "correct methods" and the better I am able to use whatever methods best support, affirm, and nurture my students as they respond, learn, and grow.

Yet I am struggling. I am still shaping my ideas about teaching, and I'm learning about teaching every single day that I teach. It is messy work, and I change my mind a lot. I have had different class outlines and different expectations, different grading procedures every year that I've taught so far. Not everything I've tried has worked, and I have experimented with methods that I will probably never use again.

However, the nonsuccesses are an essential part of the process of my own learning; I'd like to think that the number of different attempts can only attest to the extent of my concern and respect for my students. And I have a feeling that my search for ways to let students' voices be heard and their responses respected is not close to being over. As messy as it may be, I enjoy the challenge of being a response-centered teacher, because of the rich learning and exploration it provides me, within an attitude that respects the most precious of all mysteries above all else.

THE FAMILY RELATIONSHIPS UNIT

During our first sessions together at our summer retreat, I worked with Janice, my cooperating teacher, to plan a literature unit in which students would have a prominent voice in the interpretation and response to texts, and in which student learning was determined not by achievement on objective multiple-choice or fill-in-the-teacher's-words tests, but by their demonstration of having created knowledge from interaction with the texts.

Everything we planned for that particular unit on family relationships was deliberate (see Chapter 6, Appendix A). We discussed each day's activities thoroughly and planned the lessons to accomplish our goals for the students. However, despite trends toward outcome-based instruction, in this unit we purposely left *undefined* the outcomes of the learning. Our goals were stated in process terms instead: Students would identify their prior knowledge about the topic, compare their ideas with those of their peers, and then read several short stories, poems, and a novel that would, we hoped, prompt them to expand or stretch their conceptual or personal understandings of "family." Again, we were operating on the assumption that the *students* brought the content to the classroom with them; we could not define what we did not know. We thought if we truly respected their experience and knowledge, and allowed all students to shape their new meanings in light of their personal experience and connection with the texts, the learning that would take place would simply be too vast and diverse to define or prescribe. All students, beginning in different places, would learn according to their needs and abilities, and so also end up in different places.

To help students call up their prior knowledge, images, and impressions about our focus word, *family,* we tried a technique that the teacher-research group had used at our summer retreat while defining our response-centered approach: Patricia Carini's "word reflection" (Traugh, 1985), in which participants write down words, phrases, and thoughts that they associate with a specified word or concept. On the board we listed items from the class members' lists and came up with a collective reflection. As students offered items from their individual lists, they expanded on one another's thoughts, and, just as had happened with the teacher group, the students got a sense of what a broad set of experiences the class held claim to. For instance, after they had the "main" family relationships listed on the board—mother, father, brothers and sisters—one student piped up and reminded us, "Not everyone has two parents who are married, ya know. We have to add stepmother and stepfather, too." Students' responses to the reflection appear in Figure 5.1.

I probably could have anticipated many of the responses students offered through this process. Our students were mostly the products of middle-class parents in a fairly stable midwestern com-

Figure 5.1. A seventh-grade class's word reflection on the word *family*.

Relatives (relationships)

Mom and Dad	Stepmom and	Aunts and Uncles
Sisters and Brothers	Stepdad	
Cousins	Stepsisters and Half-brothers	
	Grandparents	

Things we know some families do together

Trips	Family Sports	Shopping
Family reunions	Get-togethers	Holidays
Celebrations	Watching T.V.	Movies
Church	Sunday Brunch	Have parties
Hobbies	Supper	Bike rides

Other images, ideas, and feelings we associate with family

Fights	Presents	"Family Car"
Pets	Laughing	Blood Types
Marriage	Babies	Houses
Divorce	Love	the Cleavers
Rules	Last names	the Brady Bunch
Sayings	Traditions	Jobs, School
Togetherness	Chores	Favoritism
Lectures	Punishments	Bills, taxes
Embarrassment		

munity, and their reflections turned out to be fairly predictable. Janice and I could have brainstormed a number of common images ourselves, put them on the overhead projector, and talked about them with the students. But as we planned and taught this unit, it was important to us that the students articulate and claim this knowledge for themselves. Part of the intention of this activity was definitely to build trust. We thought that listening to the responses that came from their own mouths and minds would give them ownership of the learning and assure them that they were the ones responsible for the knowledge-making in this classroom.

The family relationships unit continued with an activity in which class members discussed and wrote definitions of the word *family*. Students were shown a model definition and then asked to

try to articulate their understandings about family in one clear definition. After a few minutes of personal brainstorming, students
formed small groups. They were instructed to share their personal
definitions and then either adopt one for the group or formulate
a new one on which everyone could agree. As each group read
its definition to the whole class, someone within or outside the
group would bring up some point that would contradict what had
been written. Groups tried to revise their definitions to be all-
encompassing, sometimes with humorous results. What resulted
were ridiculously vague definitions such as this one, contributed by
one of the student groups: *"Family:* a group of people that may or
may not live together, may or may not care for each other, and may
or may not be related by blood, marriage, or adoption."

The point of this exercise was not to get the whole class to come
to a unified conclusion about how families should be defined; in a
time in which that question is being debated at all levels, that would
have been a ridiculous expectation. In some classes, a spoken consensus was reached: that the concept of "family" is *complex*—a
healthy, open-minded viewpoint, indeed. In other classes, some students made a stand that family types that did not "fit the definition"
should not be considered families. In any case, the activity served its
purpose, which was to help students identify their prior knowledge,
compare it with that of their classmates, and then redefine or create
their own new knowledge. And at no point were students told a
"right answer" by a teacher. The class members' own views were
central to the activity, and indeed were the only views that counted.

After these two introductory activities, the unit continued with
the reading of several short stories and poems that had a focused
family relationship at the heart of the plot or theme. As we introduced the stories to the students, we reminded them only of the
family relationship that would be featured and guided them by encouraging them to see what they could learn about family relationships from reading. We consciously tried not to guide students to
specific teacher-chosen understandings of the texts, and we tried to
keep our own agendas out of the reading experience.

During the days of reading the literature, we almost always sur-
rounded the reading of the text by reflections and written responses
that invited class members to think about the text or family relationship in light of their own experience. For instance, after reading
"One-Shot Finch," a chapter from *To Kill a Mockingbird* in the
school's literature anthology (Lee, 1985), we asked the seventh-
graders to write a description of Atticus as a father. They could de-

scribe any aspect of Atticus's person or character that they could visualize or imagine after reading the chapter. The description was followed by the students' freewriting about their relationship with their own father or other important adult male in their lives. Writing here was used as a form of thinking through a personal relationship, something which some of these 12-year-olds admitted they had never done before.

Other response activities we tried included illustrating characters and events; choosing "the most important" (*each student's* "most important") idea in a text and creating a visual representation of that idea; completing prompted writings and freewritings that encouraged students to tell what they thought as they read and to make connections with characters, events, words, and ideas. Class discussion was a powerful tool as well, although I found it difficult at first to facilitate the students' discussion without becoming the *focus* of that discussion, the main contributor to whom the students would look for "correct" opinions and answers.

At the end of a week of reading and responding to stories and poems, Janice and I asked students to produce a written response to the activities that served as evidence of the learning they had accomplished. Some of the students' responses are recorded in Chapter 1. Other students not cited in Chapter 1 wrote equally well about the connections that they had made to the texts we had read. Several directly cited growth in their thinking about family—that they had come to understand a wider definition of family relationships through the literature we shared.

Janice and I did not "test" the students on these short stories and poems. We did not give "pop quizzes." Instead, we made ourselves trust their voices, as those voices were expressed through their various responses. At the end of the unit, we were convinced that most of the seventh-graders had created meaning from their interactions with literature in this response-centered classroom, and that the family relationships unit had been successful. Janice and I had done our best to keep students' responses at the center of our focus. We tried to respect and affirm the ideas of individuals, and we did not promote our own opinions as superior to any other reader's. And as classroom groups, the students had "passed" our family relationships literature unit with flying colors.

But then, within each of those shining classroom groups, hid a few others—the nonparticipants: the ones who remained silent during the discussions and wrote brief, impersonal, uninvolved reactions and reflections to literature; the ones who doodled, or slept, or made snide remarks during our "meaning-full" interactions with texts. There weren't many of them, but what was to be done about them? Is *no* response a valid response? Perhaps . . . occasionally. What if no response is the *only* response *ever* offered by a student? How does a teacher with the best intentions to trust and respect students keep from being taken advantage of by the students who just don't care? These were the questions that remained with me after my student teaching experience with Janice and those seventh-graders ended that winter. These were the questions left unresolved as I moved into my own teaching position and began my own odyssey as a response-centered teacher.

READER RESPONSE LOGS

The question of the nonparticipants became of even greater importance to me when I began my first solo teaching experience. Like most new teachers, I was a little overwhelmed when I realized that all those students were completely *my* responsibility. Certainly, the knowledge that some students were falling through the cracks was troubling enough. But now, those students were becoming intimidating. Somehow, the uncooperative ones hadn't seemed so threatening to me when Janice was there, always in the room, ready to back me up, her mere presence "persuading" most of the doubtful students to go along with what I was doing. Encouraged by my youth and inexperience, though, the noncooperators were now bold as ever, and, to be honest, I was a bit terrified of them. I didn't much feel like risking a lot of whole-class response activities, like the ones I was able to try during the family relationships unit, when a few uncompassionate students could make the whole thing go to pieces. I searched for an answer to my dilemmas.

When I read Nancie Atwell's description of her experience with reader-response logs in her book *In the Middle* (1987), I knew it was a method that fit the ideals of our response-centered approach. I also thought that it might offer a workable solution to my struggle with the nonparticipating type of student. I thought students would be more motivated to participate, since the logs allow the flexibility for each student to respond freely and in informal language to the texts he or she encounters with some degree of privacy—safety. Also, there is greater accountability for individuals, since it is obvious to the teacher what each student's contribution has been. In the end, I chose to use a reader-response log as the primary responding method in my class, and I just hoped that my trusting and valuing of students' voices would win them over.

In my classroom, reader-response logs look a lot like Nancie Atwell described them. They are housed in spiral notebooks provided by students, and the entries consist of periodic written—and sometimes drawn—reactions to the texts the students read during our reading days.

From the beginning, I noticed that students interacted differently with their logs. Some students wrote summaries of the texts they read but never went into much more depth in their writing than saying "I like this" or "I hate this." Other students, though, interacted on a more personal level within the reading log format.

One eighth-grade student, who kept her reader-response log faithfully, wrote in her log as intimately as one might in a diary. Her text became a testimony to the power that reading a novel—*Sati* by Christopher Pike (1990)—had for her:

LOG ENTRY #21 Sati pp. 1–120

Sati is a woman Michael, the main character, found sitting on a road on his way to Los Angeles. She rode with him.

Sati claims to be God. Michael is unsure of her but very compelled to listen at the same time.

She indeed has a gift. During her "meetings" with various people she helps them. She helps everyone in different ways; knowledge, healing, mental understanding, etc.

At the beginning of every meeting they take a moment of "rest." During this "rest" they encountered a strange feeling of peace and harmony.

This is by far the most intriguing, different novel I have ever read. I would recommend it to anyone who wants to understand. Everyone who will try.

LOG ENTRY #22 Sati pp. 175–276 (end)

You can't imagine the power of Christopher Pike's novel, Sati. It was the most enchanting novel I have ever read!

Sati was right. Words just can't describe the power some things in life have on us. Silence is the only way. Never mind. I can not presume you've read it and if you haven't you wouldn't understand. But of course, likewise if you have, you would understand. Anyway, whether you have read it or not does not matter but that I have and I wish everyone could have the same oppurtunity. They can.

A quote from the back cover, "SATI—For all who meet her Sati will change everything. Sati may change everything for you."

And she has.

Another eighth-grader read the newspaper regularly during our personal reading days and used his log writing as a way of thinking through articles he'd read, such as the two sports news articles he discusses here:

LOG ENTRY Dec 2 Star Tribune
I'm really kind of mad that John Smiley is leaving us. he really was good I guess he likes pitching in the national league. He must like to hit. What really stinks is that He gets so dang much money for pitching. I think they should regulate how much money every team can spend. that would be alot better for us and the players. Then we won't have to pay so much for tickets. Then they're attendance will go [up]. I really wish they would get smart.

LOG ENTRY Dec 4 Star Tribune
I'm really very glad that Kirby signed with us and that he gave 30,000 dollars to kids that cant [sic] afford to make it to twins games. Hes the greatest twin that minnesota ever had. And so many people would have been mad if he left too, although 30 million is way to [sic] much money.

Another log charts a student's exploration of several genres. He evaluates both *Willow* (Drew, 1988) and *Encyclopedia Brown Shows the Way* (Sobol, 1972), discussing what he likes in a book, what he finds "boring," and what "drives him crazy":

LOG ENTRY 12/4/92
Today I continued reading my book, "Willow." I read from pages 40–65.

During this part, Willow was given Elora Danan again. He must find Fin Raziel. She will bring them to a safe place and bring down the Nockmaar Army. On the way Elora ran out of milk. They had to stop by a tavern and get some fresh milk. Once he got in there, people were throwing and yelling insults at him. He had to hide. Then he slipped through a loose board in the wall. He saw Madmartigan hurrying and trying to get some women's clothing on. The woman next to him started screaming when she saw Willow. Suddenly her husband came crashing through the door. And the rest is kind of dumb. This book is beginning to become boring. I might stop reading.

LOG ENTRY 12/5/92

Today I read "Willow." I read for 30 minutes. I read through pages 66–83. I don't know why I continued reading this book. Maybe I didn't want to leave a book unfinished.

This is one of my favorite parts of the book. This part they had already found Fin Raziel. Once they came back from shore from the island Raziel was banashed [sic] too, they were captured by the Nockmaar Army. The Army didn't know it was Raziel because she was turned into a animal when she was banashed.

Madmartigan, the two Brownies, Willow, and Fin Raziel were taken to a Nockmaar camp atop a snow covered mountain. When they were locked up, Willow tried to turn Raziel backed [sic] to a human being with the wand Cherlindrea had given him. Instead he turned her into a crow. They they escaped from the baby. Sorsha is the evil Queen's daughter. But when Madmartigan saw her he fell in love. I can't wait to see what happens.

LOG ENTRY 12/6/92

Today I started reading "Encyclopedia Brown" shows the way. I read pages 1–30 for 45 minutes. I read the Case of the Growling Dog, Red Harmonica, Knockout Artist, and the Headless Runner. This is the second book I read from the Encyclopedia Brown series. I like these books because it is fun trying to solve th[e cases]. Some of my friends think it is a 2nd grader book. But I think you're never too old too read any kind of book. Especially any kind of mystery book.

LOG ENTRY 12/7/92

Today I read for 30 minutes. I started on page 31 and ended on page 53. I read through the Case of the Reward Money, the Case of the Tooth Puller, The Case of the Girl Shortstop. I like reading these books because it is fun trying to solve the cases. I read all of these books when I was in 4th grade. But I like reading them again. The cases are easy to solve but you have to pay attention to the details.

LOG ENTRY 12/10/92

Today I read for 30 minutes. I read Encyclopedia Brown Shows the Way. I finished it today. I read the Case of the Rattlesnake's Rattle, World Traveler, and the Lady Ghost. My favorite case to solve in the whole book was the Rattlesnake's Rattle. It was about a boy who watched a Rattlesnake at [and] someone had stolen the rattle. It was easy to solve though. The thing that I don't like about this book is that they should have a lot more characters. Well I can't wait to read the next Encyclopedia Brown book.

LOG ENTRY 12/11/92

Since I finished my Encyclopedia Brown, I needed to read something else. I read a number of magazines on the table. My favorite story was called "The Last Answer" by Hal Ellson. It was in the magazine called Read. This was a scary story. It is one of the most suspenseful stories I have ever read. One thing I don't like about it was the abrupt ending. I hate those kind of endings. They drive me crazy. I would like to know what happens. This story isn't like a fantasy story. It is really realistic. I like it a lot. I wish I could write stories like these.

As I collected the logs to read and respond to every 2 to 4 weeks, I read countless entries like these. Reader response logs seemed to bring honest, thoughtful responses out of more of my students, probably because of the informal nature of the writing and the fact that the logs provided a direct line of communication between the students and myself. What I enjoyed most was the way that logs, unlike some traditional book report formats that this method replaced, invited students to explore their own issues and agendas as well as summarize and evaluate the text. Some writers, like the first student above, personalized the reading experience; others, like the second, explored related issues; still others, like the third, constructed their own images of self-as-reader. The reader response log, in my opinion, proved to be a successful way of individualizing the curriculum for students, motivating more students to participate, and validating the response of each individual.

But what about my "nonparticipators"? Yes, sadly, there were still some logs missing from the pile each time I collected them. Some students still chose not to participate in the responding; sadly, most of these students had also chosen not to read. Reader response logs had not been the miracle cure that I had hoped for.

But, whether it was a simple result of my growing experience in the classroom or the inspiring success of the logs with the majority of my students, I began to put the "problem" of the nonparticipators in a different perspective. I think I began to separate the failures of those students from any particular method that I could hope to blame, and to identify the true failure as one of trust or of relationships. Those few students who choose not to participate in responding often don't trust or like me personally, often don't like school or trust other adults in the school, and often don't like reading. This is a little hard to accept, especially as a beginning teacher, but I suppose, since we are all human, it is to be expected that we will not always like one another. And certainly the intimacy and sense of direct communication the reader response logs offer must be as threatening to some as it is motivating to others. However, the question remains: What am I to do about them?

I do not know the answer, even now, with a few more seasons of teaching in my experience. I'm quite sure, though, that the answer does *not* lie in abandoning the attitudes of trust and respect for individuals underpinning the response-centered approach. I know that reverting to a more dictatorial approach would not do anything to build relationships that have been broken by who-knows-what kinds of negative experiences, impressions, and attitudes. Although I am relying again on my intuition here, I think that my best approach will be to continue to trust and invite students to respond, and to listen with respect when they do. When they're ready, maybe they'll join in the conversation; if I'm lucky, that time will come during the period I have to work with them.

EXPLAINING WHAT I MEAN BY RESPONSE

Using the response-centered approach, whether through a highly structured literature unit or through the use of reading logs in conjunction with independent reading, I see that my main task as a teacher is not to evaluate as much as it is to teach kids what I mean by "response," and then, simply, to facilitate and support their responding. Students should become the main evaluators and assessors of their own learning, but only after they understand that I, the teacher, have relinquished that power and given them the right and responsibility to take it over.

In the family relationships unit and since, I have introduced options for responding outright to students. I present a definition of response on an overhead transparency, shown in Figure 5.2, and a list of ideas, shown in Figure 5.3. In sharing my knowledge about what we are doing and why we are doing it—even with students as young as 12 and 13 years old—I feel I am empowering the students to take charge of their own learning and encouraging them to do so by assuring them that their unique responses will be respected. Besides, I think I build credibility and integrity in the eyes of my students when they see me revealing my methods to them, when they see that I am not trying to manipulate them but am trusting them with my "teacher secrets."

Defining for others "what I mean by response" has become a bit more interesting now that many students and teachers are familiar with a reader-response literature textbook series. The "response textbooks," I must admit, look a lot different from the textbooks I grew up with, which stopped the readers after each section to check for recall and understanding by answering a number of questions, to which answers were found in a special teacher's edition. The new textbooks ask students to respond to and share their answers to open-ended questions, many of which direct students back to connections with their own experiences. Predictably, colleagues and students associate my talk about response-centered teaching with the reader-response literature books; I need to do everything I can to make sure that the two never become synonymous.

Although I respect the efforts of the textbook series' authors to promote open-ended thinking and exploration of complex ideas in literature rather than focusing on surface detail, I think that the coexistence of questions on the page with real texts sends inappropriate messages to readers. The implication is that readers—teachers and students—in conversation are not capable, on their own, of identifying perfectly good—interesting, important—questions to be addressed in writing and in discussion. The implication is that the textbook writers know the best, most important questions, and number one is *the* most important question, the one readers should consider before any others. My biggest complaint is that when following the questions printed in the textbook, the readers are always following someone else's agenda, not being driven by their own needs and interests, something that only they themselves could know. As innovative as any textbook may be, it will never be personal enough for me; that instructional format in itself can never cease to be impersonal.

I guess what it comes down to is that "what I mean by response" will *always* include the element of human interaction among read-

Figure 5.2. A definition of response for use in the classroom.

---

* Is what we do naturally
* Is taking our attitudes, feelings, and reactions toward what we read (or hear or see), and DOING something with them.
* Is diverse. The way you respond to something will be different from the way your classmates and friends respond because you are a unique person . . .
  You have different
    thoughts,
    feelings,
    experiences,
    attitudes, and
    interests
  than anyone else.
* Is always "right" as long as it is honest and focused.

Figure 5.3. Suggested response formats.

	Writing	
free writing	characters' diaries	review
essay	letter to the author	original poetry
letter to a character	rewriting the ending	others?
	Illustration/Graphics	
photographs	collages	posters
cartoons	diagrams	illustrations
paintings	murals	others?
	Video/Performance	
acting out a scene	music	dance
roleplaying	mime	videotaping
audio taping	others?	

ers, between teachers and students. I operate on the assumption that the students' greatest need is *not* just to be asked the right kind of questions, but to be heard, respected, encouraged as they respond naturally, honestly to the texts they read—like "real" readers, with individuality and lives of worth and consequence.

The response-centered approach is not a miracle cure for the problems facing the literature classroom, such as unmotivated readers. However, I see it as the best of the possibilities because of its positive, individualized approach. More often than traditional approaches, which merely reward a student's ability to recall details and the teacher's opinions, ideas, and words, it demands that students operate at higher levels of thinking, analyzing, applying, and creating. The response-centered approach has nothing inherently to do with textbook series or other expensive materials, and it requires no special classroom setup, so it has been infinitely adaptable to new school and teaching environments. It also assumes the best in all students, recognizes and respects their knowledge, and motivates their inherent urge to learn because it guarantees success to all who participate thoughtfully. And for me, it offers the opportunity to be the kind of teacher I want to be—free to appreciate the beauty of the humanness of my students: "the most precious of all mysteries."

LITERATURE SELECTIONS

Drew, Wayland. (1988). *Willow.* New York: Ballantine.

Lee, Harper. (1985). One-shot Finch from *To kill a mockingbird.* In *Adventures for readers* (Book 1; pp. 98–106). Orlando, FL: Harcourt Brace Jovanovich.

Pike, Christopher. (1990). *Sati.* New York: Tom Doherty Associates.

Sobol, Donald J. (1972). *Encyclopedia Brown shows the way.* New York: Dutton.

CHAPTER 6

So That Our Students' Lives Will Be Better for Their Time Spent with Us

JANICE L. ANDERSON

I would love to have no fear, so I could be more curious.
Paul Rugroden, Grade 7

I believe that all teachers are idealists, at least at the beginning of their teaching careers, and that part of that idealism involves a wish to have a lasting impact on their students' lives. I have that wish. I had it when I began teaching, and I have it today. In my more fanciful moments, I imagine one of my students at her inauguration as president announcing to the world that her inspiration came from a poem first read to her by her seventh-grade English teacher. Or I see one of my former students speaking softly to his son, "Read, little boy, read. My seventh-grade English teacher said it's the most important thing for you to do. And she was right. So read, little boy, read." I always smile at these fantasies; sometimes they are so real I almost weep. And I have to believe that other teachers have them, too, in those rare moments when we have time for reflections and daydreams. As teachers, we yearn to produce a kind of resonance in our students' lives. We want the messages to continue to sound, to intensify over time and enrich our students' lives for many years. We want the messages to be loud and rich and deep so that our students' lives will be better for their time spent with us.

As an active English teacher, I wanted my students to hear not just my voice, but the voices of the great writers. I wanted them to know and understand the messages of all those people whose writing has made an impact on our lives, our culture, and our world. I wanted those messages, so vital and important in my life, to resonate through the lives of my students. It wasn't happening.

It didn't seem to matter what I did. I recognized learning styles; asked how and why questions instead of what and where questions; used cooperative learning groups; encouraged higher-level thinking skills, creative thinking skills, critical thinking skills. It didn't seem to matter what I did—the students still did the same things. Some of them performed whatever task I required of them diligently and wholeheartedly. Some of them performed the task minimally. Some of them performed the task not at all, but instead observed all of this rich variety with curiosity and amusement. And some of my students . . . just slept. Individuals may have drifted from one group to another according to which of the latest techniques I had adopted, but the proportions remained static, and so did my feelings of frustration and even despair.

The first inkling I had that there might be something out there that would work for me was in the North Dakota Council of Teachers of English newsletter. An article by Barb described a lesson in which a class read a piece of literature together, wrote a response to it, discussed their responses in small groups, expanded that discussion to the large group, and then, perhaps, wrote a formal paper on the piece of literature. I thought, "Wow!" It seemed so simple, so easy, so natural. Of course, I immediately began second-guessing myself. It's too simple, too easy, too natural! Who would be in control here? What about the discussion questions? What about my study guide? When would we do the vocabulary words? What would the principal say? Who would be in charge here? That copy of the newsletter remained on top of my desk for 2 years. I would occasionally retrieve it from the bottom of a pile of papers, review it, and repeat the process of enthusiasm, wonder, questioning, and putting it off.

During this time I was hearing talk of new teaching techniques associated with such names as response writing, Reader's Workshop, and Nancie Atwell (1987). Each was supposed to involve students more in the literature assigned in the classroom. I was once again curious but didn't have the time or energy to investigate further.

That investigation was initiated for me by a colleague in my school, Joyce, when she caught me in the hall one day and asked if I would be interested in working on a project with her and Barb. It involved response-centered language arts classrooms. I quickly agreed to this collaboration and became a part of a project that changed my classroom forever.

I was once asked, in a job interview, if I ran my classroom as a democracy or a dictatorship. I couldn't answer the question. The interviewers clearly wanted a "dictatorship" response, and I couldn't give it to them. I wanted to say "democracy," but I knew that wasn't completely accurate either. So the three of us stared at each other until I stumbled through some gobbledygook answer that didn't really mean anything. I didn't get the job. What I did get was an opportunity to consider that question—dictatorship or democracy?—over a long period of time.

It's an important question with only unsatisfactory answers unless one changes the framework of the question. A classroom that is run like a dictatorship invests the teacher with all the power, knowledge, and information. It doesn't recognize the power, knowledge, and information that the students bring into that room. A democratic classroom, on the other hand, seems to treat everyone as equals. The students have equal authority with the teacher. The knowledge, the information, the view of the world that each carries to the classroom is seen as equal to that of the teacher. This is very empowering to the students, but without some kind of recognizable leadership, this classroom may quickly fall into chaos. Obviously, neither answer is appropriate. For me, the question wasn't appropriate either. I needed a new question with a new answer. Reader response was it.

Reader response works for me because it acknowledges each class member as a valuable contributor to the understanding of a piece of work. Everyone has power as a contributor, and everyone has the right to take away his or her understanding of a piece of literature. The teacher is not the sole source of all the good ideas; the teacher becomes the guide, mediator, or facilitator.

This became very clear to me during a small-group discussion of the word *family*. We were preparing to begin a unit on family (see Appendix A) and were exploring the idea of family. One group of four seventh-grade students almost came to blows trying to arrive at a definition of the word. They agreed that members of a family needed to care for each other and support each other. The problem was one boy's insistence that families also fight together. The discussion quickly descended to the "they do too/they do not" stage with voices alternating between screeches and growls, faces darkening past pink to sweaty red, eyes glowering beneath lowered heads, and hands balled into tight fists. I approached the group and asked what the problem was. Susie said, "Loving families don't fight." Joe said, "My family does!" Clearly, each student came into this argument with a strong point of view based on his or her life experiences. I could easily have sided with either student, probably depending on how things were going in my own family. Instead, I asked Susie a simple question. "Have you ever had a disagreement with your mother? Did you argue?" Susie answered, "Yeah, but . . ." and the argument returned to a discussion. The students were able to integrate the family fight into their definition of a loving and supportive family. This in turn led to a deeper and more truthful understanding of the literature in our family unit. I didn't need to be the source of the answer to this question. I didn't dictate the correctness of any group's answer. Rather, I facilitated compromise and integration of diverse viewpoints while demonstrating respect for each individual's ideals. My job had shifted. I was no longer the "great purveyor of deep meaning," a title that so often seems attached to the words *English teacher.* By recognizing the truth of each student's world, I was able to discard that title and become a fellow traveler in the world of literature. When the class continued our family unit by reading the novel *Incident at Hawk's Hill* by Allan W. Eckert (see Appendix B), we were free to explore the literature and the issues without the constraints of a study guide's right and wrong answers. The response packet gave form to our discussions and a forum for students to explore their own realities.

Today I reflect on the art of literature and respond to it. I require my students to do this. I do it with them. We test the truth of the art on our own realities; sometimes accepting, sometimes discarding it; often setting it aside to be further examined at another time. It seems to me that this process of accepting students as individuals with a world view, of respecting their responses to literature as valid and honest, and of sharing the responsibility for the involvement with the art of literature with them must produce a greater resonance in their lives. That is why I continue struggling toward a response-centered classroom.

GUIDELINES FOR A RESPONSE-CENTERED CLASSROOM

So how did I get there? How do I continue on this path? How do I resist the temptation to go backward and not forward? What makes my classroom a safe place for students to respond to literature rather than look for the "right" answer? I have discovered a few guidelines that help me answer these questions.

One of the messages that is often heard in my classroom is that language has power. Last April, Cyndy had heard about her need for Clearasil treatment from Nathan one too many times. She responded by slapping his desk with her open hand and shouting in his face,

"Stop that or I'll have Jacob take care of you at the store," and bursting into tears. Nathan accused Cyndy of threatening him and the fight was on. I sent Cyndy to the bathroom to get a drink and cool off, and Nathan and I sat down for a visit. He explained what had happened very frankly. I responded with one of my favorite lines, "You know, Nathan, words have power," all the time looking him straight in the eye.

Nathan answered, without a pause, "You know, Mrs. A., you oughtta be a 'feelosopher.' You really gotta knack for this feelings stuff."

"Right, Nathan," I said. "What about Cyndy?"

"OK, Mrs. A. I'll apologize, but I better not see Jacob hanging around."

He did apologize. And Cyndy did not request Jacob's services.

The language and words in a response-centered classroom are usually positive, polite, and courteous. This is not only required of the students, but also of me. The power of positive, courteous language in school plays an important role in acknowledging and encouraging students to be active learners. It encourages the openness and trust necessary to share individual versions of the world. It allows students' natural curiosity to assert itself, because they trust that they will not be put down or embarrassed. As Paul Rugroden, one of my seventh-grade students, stated so powerfully, "I would love to have no fear, so I could be more curious." If students can operate in a safe environment, they will feel more comfortable and be more willing to take the risks necessary to be truly deep thinkers.

As a teacher, I must open my own mind in a positive way to the possibilities of what my students are really saying. I must help them search for their nugget of truth and affirm their efforts and meanings. And I must welcome each student's responses in order to help every individual to acknowledge his or her abilities. Sometimes this is very difficult, especially when student responses seem shallow or superficial. Searching for a positive comment that may elicit a more thoughtful response in the future can be difficult, but it is required in order to encourage the students' trust in the teacher and belief in their own abilities.

My approach to students' work must be as respectful as my approach to the students themselves. Writing a thought or an idea down on paper is truly scary. Writing something down makes it real; it takes that idea from the private darkness of each person's mind into the light of the community. The world can't deny it, and neither can the individual who created it. The risk that a young person is taking when he or she writes a personal response of any kind must be acknowledged and affirmed before the teacher moves on to questions, criticisms, or compliments. This is an important opportunity for us, as teachers and significant adults, to affirm our students' courage.

My approach to literature has changed, too. I have found that I must acknowledge differences in interpretation to my students and that I am exploring the artists' ideas along with my classes. I still try to establish a basic understanding of the concrete details of a piece, such as historical background, form, and vocabulary. I also try to let students know that an author's work doesn't always mean the same thing or have the same value; that the work doesn't remain static even though it is finished; that each individual's interaction with it necessarily changes it into something new and different. Students need to know that these ideas, to some so foreign, are OK. I must encourage this interchange between reader, writer, and literature. These opportunities allow and encourage the deeper processing that may create that resonance that we yearn for.

A final challenge involves my approach to the various parties who have an interest in what goes on in my classroom. Teachers, colleagues, parents, and administrators all have a valid reason to question this process and to ask, "Are they really doing anything?" That's their job! And they would be failing in their job if they didn't ask. For my part, I need to be able to demonstrate that this is a valid technique for teaching reading, writing, and literature. Handing them the references list for this book is a very concrete place to start. Then they can see that this type of learning is thoroughly grounded in respected research and theory.

I believe that it's very important to stress the hard work that these students do with this process and to explain to all what students have actually accomplished. I try to acknowledge my class as a community of learners and to encourage others to reinforce the risk-taking that occurs in this atmosphere. I remind the curious that this is a process that helps to create able learners from students who may have opted out of the learning process, encourages those who may have been too timid to participate in the risks of active learning, and affirms those who have been leaders in the classroom, maybe even forcing those leaders to participate at a deeper, more meaningful level. I demonstrate these skills by sharing the work of my students (with their permission) and freely allowing others to visit my classroom so that they may see my students in action.

HELPING STUDENTS RESPOND

When I meet my seventh-grade students in the fall, they usually have not done much actual free exploration of literature. The range of writing abilities always surprises me. My first tasks are to make my students comfortable with creating responses and to make them aware of my expectations. We start with writing a free response to a selection from our literature book. This requires a lot of "safe" talk—that what they write is OK, that anything they have to say is OK, that any question is OK, that they are OK. My only requirement is that their writing be at least one-half page long, and that, yes, that means down to the middle hole in their paper and that, yes, it is okay to write more that one-half page. Some students will read their responses to the class, and we will discuss the differences and similarities between responses without indicating in any way that one is more right than another. It is great fun for me to watch the cautious faces become curious, questioning, and more trusting.

In the first months of school, I will actively assign different "types" of responses. These may include a questioning response, a personal experience response, a visual response, a letter response, a "become one of the characters" response, a poetry response, even group responses. We practice these responses in the first 5 to 7 days of our family unit. Our first book report, a friendly letter to me (see Appendix C), includes a response paragraph. The level of noise increases steadily in my classroom. The "shop talk" among the students is exciting. Many students are very comfortable with one "type" of response and challenged by another. That's good. For me, the visual responses are the most fun, because they allow nonverbal students to express their interpretation of literature in ways never allowed before. Amazing things happen when we take away the boundaries set by words for these students.

After we have practiced a variety of possibilities, I do away with the "types" and usually assign a "free" response. This usually occurs about the seventh day of our family unit. Once again, we have a lot of "safe talk," but students quickly learn that any "type" of response is truly OK. At this point, I require more length in their writing, begin asking the students more questions about their responses, encourage them to support their ideas with evidence from the literature, and generally move toward more traditional writing skills within the response form.

Students use response writing in connection with many different traditional English classroom selections. They respond to all different types of literature including poetry, short stories, longer novels, and nonfiction. Sometimes students respond to characters in the literature (see Appendix D). By spring my students are very comfortable with this format, feel free to express themselves fully, and write at greater length with more structure and more precise ideas. They truly seem to be actively engaged in their learning and to enjoy participating in a piece of literature.

ENERGY, JOY, AND RESPECT: THEN RESONANCE

Do my students learn more than students in a more traditional classroom? I don't know; we certainly haven't taken any tests to prove that they do. I do know that they are excited when they come to English class. They are noisy and energetic and very verbal. Many students demand to know "what are we doing today?" They'll let me know that spelling is boring, vocabulary is OK, grammar they understand, but they would really like to read another one of those good stories—like we did the other day. And I guess that is what I was searching for—enthusiasm, excitement, joy, noise—that shouts volumes for students—that this is fun and enjoyable. I believe that this joyful learning, for it is learning, begins with a rather ponderous-sounding philosophy called response-centered classrooms. Belief in this philosophy leads to respect—respect for the students, for me, and for the literature. I believe that from respect, joy, and excitement will spring the kind of resonance for which we English teachers are searching.

APPENDIX A
Families: Yours and Mine
A Part of an Interdisciplinary Curriculum
Centered on a Response-Centered Approach to Literature

Deb and I wrote this unit at the beginning of her student teaching experience in my classroom (see Chapter 5). This was our first practical application of our summer's research with Barb, Karla, Joyce, and Teresa. Like most first tries, it isn't perfect and has, of course, been changed and modified each year. However, I use it even today in a form very close to this as the first unit of the year. It works very well as an introduction to response writing because it deals with a universal element, family, and it includes a wide variety of response experiences. After this unit is completed, I refrain from being as directive in my response assignments.

GOALS:
1. Students will explore family relationships through various forms of literature.
2. Students will explore their own intellectual and emotional response to literature.
3. Students will consider and value their own and another's experiences in response to literature.

TEXTS:
Adventures for Readers: Book One
Literature and Language: Red Level

LITERATURE SELECTIONS:

Fathers: "One-Shot Finch" by Harper Lee (1985)
            "Those Winter Sundays" by Robert Hayden (1985)
Mothers: "The Courage That My Mother Had" by Edna St. Vincent Millay (1985)
Siblings: "Sled" by Thomas E. Adams (1985)
            "Those Saturday Afternoons" by James Baldwin (1985)
The Whole: "Home" by Gwendolyn Brooks (1985)
            "Nikki-Rosa" by Nikki Giovanni (1973)
            "The Rescue of the Perishing" by William Saroyan (1985)
Seniors: "My Grandmother Would Rock Quietly and Hum" by Leonard Adame (1985)
            "old age sticks" by e. e. cummings (1994)

SCHEDULE:
Day 1: Word reflection on the word *family.*
Day 2: Create a definition of family.
        Brainstorm a list of the characteristics of a family.
        Write a dictionary-type definition of family. (I write a dictionary definition on the board as a model—*horse* is a good example.)
        Small groups: Using each definition as a resource, write a purpose statement for families. Why do they exist? Share with the large group.
Day 3: "One-Shot Finch"
        Prewriting: Draw a picture with words of your father or an important older male in your life.

Response: Pretend you are Scout. Draw a picture with words of your family. Be sure that you are Scout.

Day 4: "Those Winter Sundays"

Response: List the things you understand about this poem and those things you don't understand.

Small groups: Review and discuss responses. Try to reach a consensus on the questions you have. This will be the basis for our large-group discussion.

Writing assignment: Compare/contrast "Those Winter Sundays" and "One-Shot Finch."

Day 5: Discuss comparison and contrast papers.

Response: Using all the knowledge we've produced this week around the word *family* and our impressions of fathers or male leaders in our lives, respond to a story and/or poem we've read.

Day 6: "The Courage That My Mother Had"

Response: Respond to this poem. Your response does not have to be in words. You may use any type of written response.

Day 7:

Small groups: Create a visual representation of the poem. Your visual representation may have words, but they should not be the central focus of your work. Your thoughtful reasoning is important. These will be posted in the room, and you will share your work and explain your thinking to the large group.

Homework: Create a poem about your mother or some important older female in your life. You may use "The Courage That My Mother Had" as a model if you wish.

Day 8: "Sled"

Read aloud.

Response: Respond to the story. You may use any of the kinds of response we have explored so far, or you may create your own.

Day 9: "Those Saturday Afternoons"

Read aloud.

Response: Respond to this story as if you are one of the brothers.

Day 10: "My Grandmother Would Rock Quietly and Hum"
       "old age sticks"

Read both poems aloud.

Response: Respond to one poem. Your response could include difficulties, things that make sense to you, and images the poetry creates in your mind and thoughts.

Small groups: (I arrange students in small groups according to poem chosen.) Share responses. Choose one problem—the one considered most important to your group for complete understanding of the poem. Try to solve the problem. Be prepared to discuss the problem and the solution with the class. Discuss common understandings and thoughts and be prepared to present those to the class also. Presentations and individual contributions to the group will be observed and graded.

Day 11: "Home"
"Nikki-Rosa"
Respond to one of these poems.
Discuss family portrait project. You will each create at least three "word pictures" of different family members, using either poetry or prose. You could use any of our selections as a model if you wish.

Day 12: "The Rescue of the Perishing"
Response: Compare/contrast with your original definition of family.

Day 13: Start projects. Bring materials.

Day 14, 15: Continue work on projects; present projects; segue into novel.

Novel Choices:
Jacob Have I Loved by Katherine Paterson (1980)
Incident at Hawk's Hill by Allan W. Eckert (1971)
Maniac McGee by Jerry Spinelli (1990)

APPENDIX B
Incident at Hawk's Hill

This is a novel unit that I often use after the family unit. I include it in this chapter as an example of how I use response writing in a novel unit. Grading response packets such as this one is a difficult problem. Generally, students will receive two grades. One grade is for completing each response to its full length with good thinking and effort evident. Students then star the response they consider their best and have an opportunity to revise and polish it. They receive a second grade for their starred response.

These are the directions given to the students on the first pages of their packet. The packet also includes five to seven blank sheets for recording their work.

We will be reading the novel *Incident at Hawk's Hill* by Allan W. Eckert in class during the next few weeks. We will also do a number of activities along with our reading. You will each receive a packet that should be in class every day along with your book.

The class will be divided into groups. During the reading of the book, every student will write several responses to the novel. Students will share these responses in their groups. Each group will be responsible for making a presentation to the class. The purpose of this presentation is to *teach* the class a particular section of the book. This presentation will include information that is important in the novel and a vocabulary list from that section. Your group should design a teaching lesson with the best teaching methods you know. We will also be doing some additional research into topics that are associated with this novel.

You will be responsible for doing five responses during this unit. They should be in this packet, which should come to class every day along with your book. The first response will be a cover prediction. At least three of the other five should be in written form and be at least one-half page long. You may do more than five if you wish.

Suggestions for responses include:

    Free response

    Observations on gossip and the role it plays in our lives

    Poetry

    Letters

    Predicting an ending

    Comic strips

    Diary or journal of one of the main characters

    News stories

    Radio shows

    Responding to a character

    Music

    Poetry

    Any response of your creation. Please check with me if you have a question about something you would like to do.

APPENDIX C
Book Report: Letter to Mrs. Anderson

I include this as an example of how response writing might be used as part of a book report. My students are required to read two or three books every quarter. This type of report requires a personal response to the story. I hope that means greater involvement with the story and that, in turn, leads to more enjoyment of personal reading.

Your book report should be in letter form. Be sure to follow all proper letter-writing procedures. Your letter should contain the following items:

Salutation

Paragraph 1

>Title of book underlined
>
>Author of book
>
>Short plot summary—40 words or less—3 to 5 sentences
>
>Be sure to describe the main conflict and use the characters' names.

Paragraph 2

>Personal response—Be sure to write about some connection you made with something in the book. For example, a character that you liked or disliked, agreed with or disagreed with and why; a setting that reminded you of some experience in your own life; a situation that reminds you of something in your own experience. Use specific examples from the book to explain your ideas. This is *not* an evaluation!

Paragraph 3

>Evaluation—State if the book is good, bad, in between, sort of good or bad, and why. Use specific examples from the book to prove your point.

Closing

>Be sure to include your name and your period.

APPENDIX D
Author Unit—Cynthia Voigt

Occasionally we do author units in my classroom. In this example, students respond to a character rather than to the literature as a whole. Voigt's books are especially well suited for this since she creates powerful characters who are forced to face real-life problems and who must grow and change in order to come to terms with them. Students enjoy getting to know a character very well. This type of response encourages students to know Voigt's characters intimately. Students actually do two assignments in this unit: a response packet and a book report. Both are included here.

*I . . . suspect that it is normal to be, like an iceberg, more
than you seem to be, to be not only what you seem to be.*
                                                        —Cynthia Voigt

Cynthia Voigt creates characters that are like icebergs. There's a lot that we see very easily—like the iceberg, we see all that is above the water, all that Voigt shows us. But she also hides a lot about her characters—puts it under the water—and lets us discover it as we read along in her books. Our focus when we read her books will be to discover so much about one character that we feel that we know him/her personally and that we can become that character.

RESPONSE ASSIGNMENT
Choose one character from the book by Voigt you have chosen to read. Choose one that is important to the story. Respond to that character at least four times during your reading of the book. At least two of your responses must be in writing. The other responses may be written or in any other form (illustrations, cartoons, sketches, etc.). You may respond more than four times if you wish. Be sure that you are responding to the character as he/she is revealed to you in the story. Use your information about character development in any way that seems appropriate. You will be handing in these responses as part of your book report.

BOOK REPORT
Pretend you are the character in the book and create a response which is about *you* as that character. Suggestions follow. If you wish to create something else, check with your teacher first. Be sure that your work reveals specific things about you, the character, and how you feel about this portrayal of yourself.
Suggestions:
  1. Write a letter to Cynthia Voigt explaining how you feel about her portrayal of you. Use correct friendly letter form.
  2. Write a journal entry explaining the events of the story from your point of view.
  3. Write a poem about being written about.
  4. Create a conversation with Cynthia Voigt in which you compliment or criticize her way of writing about you.
  5. Create an editorial cartoon in which you say something about the way people are portrayed in novels. Write an editorial to go with it. Use your portrayal as evidence to support your position.

6. Create an advertising campaign for your book using you, the character, to promote it. Be sure you have visual and written sections in your campaign.

LITERATURE SELECTIONS

Adame, Leonard. (1985). My grandmother would rock quietly and hum. In *Adventures for readers* (Book 1). Orlando, FL: Harcourt Brace Jovanovich.

Adams, Thomas E. (1985). Sled. In *Adventures for readers* (Book 1). Orlando, FL: Harcourt Brace Jovanovich.

Baldwin, James. (1985). Those Saturday afternoons. In *Adventures for readers* (Book 1). Orlando, FL: Harcourt Brace Jovanovich.

Brooks, Gwendolyn. (1985). Home. In *Adventures for readers* (Book 1). Orlando, FL: Harcourt Brace Jovanovich.

cummings, e. e. (1994). Old age sticks. In *Literature and language.* Evanston, IL: McDougal, Littell.

Eckert, Allan W. (1971). *Incident at Hawk's Hill.* Boston: Little, Brown.

Giovanni, Nikki. (1973). Nikki-Rosa. In *Ego-tripping.* New York: Hill.

Hayden, Robert. (1985). Those winter Sundays. In *Adventures for readers* (Book 1). Orlando, FL: Harcourt Brace Jovanovich.

Lee, Harper. (1985). One-shot Finch. In *Adventures for readers* (Book 1). Orlando, FL: Harcourt Brace Jovanovich.

Millay, Edna St. Vincent. (1985). The courage that my mother had. In *Adventures for readers* (Book 1). Orlando, FL: Harcourt Brace Jovanovich.

Paterson, Katherine. (1980). *Jacob have I loved.* New York: Avon.

Saroyan, William. 1985. The rescue of the perishing. In *Adventures for readers* (Book 1). Orlando, FL: Harcourt Brace Jovanovich.

Spinelli, Jerry. (1990). *Maniac McGee.* Boston: Little, Brown.

CHAPTER 7

The Dog That Barks Me Awake in the Middle of the Night Is Named Academic Rigor

KARLA SMART

I teach Principia. Commitment to response-centered teaching, in all of my work but most specifically with Principia, has changed what I do and how I think about what students do. What I ask of student groups has changed. How I open conversation about the writing students are to do has changed. How I know that students are reading for class and what that means to me have changed. How I feel about students having their own conversations rather than holding discussions to answer the questions I provide has changed. How I feel about the need for students to be doing or knowing the same things, all at the same time, has changed. The kinds of questions students ask me, and each other, have changed. And the resources, including student voices, that I want as evaluation tools have changed.

What matters most to me, in the collegiality and collaboration we six teachers have explored and continue to share, is that we intend for our students to come to what Maxine Greene (1979) calls "the release of meaning" (p. 123). What matters not at all is that we teach seventh-grade through graduate level. Nor does it matter that we teach English, or teacher education, or liberal arts courses.

I learned about Principia, a required liberal arts experience for first-year college students, in the midst of conversation about what was to become my position in secondary teacher education at a midwestern liberal arts college. Each aspect of Principia appealed to me. It is thematic. It is interdisciplinary. It is taught by faculty from across the disciplines. The interview drew out my beliefs and values as a teacher of future teachers. All the while I kept my fingers crossed and mentioned at every opportunity that I would also like to teach Principia. Little did I imagine, during the interview, that work with Principia students would one day become part of my scholarship as a teacher educator.

PRINCIPIA: AIMS, EXPECTATIONS, QUESTIONS

Principia is a semester-long course that aims to introduce students to the nature of thinking in the disciplines. Principia faculty come from nearly all departments, making immediate colleagues of poets, musicians, sociologists, philosophers, chemists, biologists, historians, English teachers, teachers of languages, women's studies scholars, theologians, teacher educators—the list goes on. As a faculty, we want students to leave Principia hungry and questioning, reflective and aware, and with clearer appreciation for the liberal arts.

There are shared expectations for us as Principia faculty. For example, we agree to select the majority of texts for our course from a common list of Principia readings, films, art and music experiences, and guest lectures. There is no textbook for Principia but rather a number of primary texts. As originally intended, it is a course in which students encounter classic texts. Increasingly, however, faculty argue in favor of more works by women and minorities.

Principia faculty are expected to include formal student writing in the course. Students generally write three to five essays during the semester, though as individual faculty we make final decisions about the writing assignments in our course.

What we share, as a Principia faculty, is commitment to liberal arts inquiry. We continue to respect the strength Principia gains through the work of individual teachers making unique choices in their classrooms. And yet, increasingly, there are students, faculty, and administrators who call for more uniformity throughout the sections.

We struggle, as a Principia faculty, with the complexity of our differences regarding what we value as knowledge and what we expect from students. These differences challenge our beliefs about approaches to classroom teaching and the assignments we plan. They challenge our understandings of the college's overall aim for co-inquiry among faculty and students, as well as the practices we initiate to make the aim a reality. Our differences are perhaps never so clear as when faculty conversation returns to a longstanding question: What is "academic rigor"?

There are ideas and questions about which we as a Principia faculty have not reached common ground. Coming to consensus in all regards is, for me, not an aim. But pursuing clearer understandings of our pedagogical perspectives remains important. The sticky questions often go unasked, just as they do in middle school or junior and senior high departments or programs: What counts as knowledge in our classrooms? What academic value is given to student voices in writing? What academic value is given to student voices in conversation and oral presentations? What counts as research and inquiry? How do we perceive the writing process, and what are the roles of teachers and student peers in that process? What are our purposes for and approaches to evaluation?

My colleagues and I choose a range of approaches in teaching Principia. Our choices come, in part, out of our individual world views and are influenced by our disciplinary expertise. Our choices, like the choices all teachers make for every course, come out of our assumptions about teaching and learning. These assumptions may or may not be explicit to ourselves, to colleagues, or to students.

COMING TO RESPONSE-CENTERED TEACHING

Aspects of response-centered teaching have been part of my thinking and teaching throughout 19 years in high school and junior college English classes and college teacher education and liberal arts courses. Writing process scholars—Ken Macrorie (1970, 1974, 1980, 1984, 1985), Peter Elbow (1973, 1981), James Moffett (1979, 1983), Janet Emig (1977), Toby Fulwiler (1982)—influenced me as a beginning teacher. Questions about writing-as-thinking led me to study creativity, theories of whole language, psycholinguistics and the reading process, and the politics of literacy. Appreciation of philosophical ideas grew as I considered Dewey's (1934) concept of experience, Maxine Greene's (1978, 1979, 1982, 1988) discussions of wide-awakeness, and Freire's (1970, 1992/1994) pedagogy of participation. Conversation with Vito Perrone invited me to consider purposes and patterns for alternative assessment. From Cecelia Traugh, I learned respect for how human is the process of education. In colleagueship with Cecelia Traugh and Patricia Carini, I discovered that collaborative teacher research can be a source of nourishment.

Just after I joined the Principia faculty, I began to meet with faculty to read and discuss feminist pedagogy. Our goals were to teach in ways that permit collaborative student work, to create openings for student voices, and to foster student ownership of knowledge.

Conversations with Barb turned up shared goals in our teaching. From the beginning, the theoretical language I most often used came from feminist scholarship and third-world pedagogy. Barb's theoretical language was rooted in reader-response literary theory and student response-centered pedagogy. We focused on the broad ideas we held in common, rather than on linguistic differences. We found that, in addition to valuing theory, we each gave high priority to asking questions about our own teaching and bringing new practices to our classrooms.

Barb drew together the six of us in authoring these stories of teaching. She recognized in each of us similar qualities of belief in the value of educational ideas, self-reflectiveness, and willingness to let our teaching practices be changed and changed again. We put aside the established languages of academic theories in favor of talk between teachers. Then, ultimately, we articulated for ourselves the philosophical beliefs we held about response-centered teaching.

THE RIGOR QUESTION IN PRINCIPIA

I will probably always ask myself each of these questions: Am I giving students enough? Am I asking enough of them? The dog that barks me awake in the middle of the night is named Academic Rigor. It is an old dog, and it really belongs to the neighbors, colleagues committed to traditional teaching and testing. But I want education to be meaningful, challenging, creative, and inspiring. I want students to be rigorous in their pursuit of knowledge. It seems the neighbor's pet knows how to make itself at home in my backyard.

It does not go unnoticed that the present Principia theme, "Freedom and Authority," names an educational issue in my life as a teacher and in the lives of students in my classroom. Traditional teaching practice—in English courses those classroom beliefs and pedagogies supported by New Criticism literary theory—continues to provide authoritative expectations and support authoritative assumptions that new practices, like the response-centered approach students and I are working with, need to face. Theorists and practitioners of new paradigms find themselves addressing old questions while at the same time shaping those most useful for reflection on their own contributions.

The question of academic rigor, for me, becomes a question of thinking. I look for rigor by looking at students' thinking. The thinking is the rigor. The questions I ask myself are these: What is the thinking? Where must I look and what must I listen to in order to know the thinking? I am interested in the meanings students make. I am interested in their responses. The thinking is there, visible in their spoken and written voices, in their visual imagery and use of metaphor and symbolism. The thinking is evident in the questions students ask—evident in a way that's different from the thinking I observe when I listen to students answer questions I have asked them. The thinking is evident in the connections students make to their own lives and to other reading—other knowledge—that they have. The rigor comes through students' participation in their own learning.

Participation, I am convinced, is most lively and meaningful to students themselves, as well as to me, when specifically invited and respected. Response-centered teaching takes seriously the idea that teachers not only ask students to be full participants in their own learning but actually permit them to be. It may require a teacher to teach students that they are expected and allowed to be responsible. I continue to learn this lesson and to find ways to carry it out. Some of what I have learned has to do with structuring a course so that my priorities are made explicit. Perhaps the greatest share has to do with trust and relationship.

STRUCTURING CLASSROOM LIFE

The tenor of classroom life is crucial in response-centered teaching because students are expected to reveal their questions and ideas. They are expected to listen to each other. Students, who know as well as I do that I am in charge, need to be able to, for the most part, forget that. They need to see that I value each of them equally, that I take each of them seriously, and that I see something unique in each of them. They need to know I will keep the promises I make to them. What this requires of me is that I share who I am with students as I come to know them. But the knowing needs to go both ways. I talk with students whenever I see them, and I remind them to take opportunities to do the same with each other.

It takes students and teachers working together to create the kind of class community that supports response-centered teaching. Collegiality requires tending. There are aspects of the pedagogy I use that foster community at the same time as they function as individual and group processes for meaning-making. What follows is a list of pedagogy and process I bring to Principia:

1. I ask students to put their chairs in a circle—a circle, not a straggly oval, not a half-moon with my chair floating on the cusp. When students can see each other and generate focus through proximity, conversation has a good chance.

2. I ask students to learn everyone's names, which, in fact, surprises some of them at first. We take time to practice names over several class periods. It is not possible to make student response a priority without first making students themselves a priority in the classroom—a priority to each other, not solely to the teacher.

3. I divide the class into student groups that remain together for an entire semester. In each group I aim for equal numbers of male and female students and, if possible, separate students who already know each other well. I aim for a fairly equal mix of students' intended disciplinary majors or favorite subject areas. As groups gather each day, I encourage use of every available inch of physical space. Groups generally spill out of the classroom, using nearby study cubbyholes and conference rooms.

4. I give student groups responsibility for keeping their own attendance records and collecting writings and visuals. The mystique of the record book disappears when students are, literally, keepers of their own education. For everyone's convenience, I store group file-folders in my office and bring them to class each day. But I do not keep back-up attendance records or my own separate record of work completed. By not keeping such records, I have no choice but to trust. By needing to trust, I keep my focus on the work of building the kind of relationships that make trusting students a safe venture for me.

5. I expect students to bring their own voices to class, adding stories and experiences, ideas and questions, creativity and critical reflections to the whole. Student response is part of the curriculum. I ask students, the first day of class, to tell personal stories relating to the course theme, signaling from the beginning that their experiences are welcomed and expected.

6. I expect students to participate in course evaluation. The student self-evaluation and course evaluation questions I pre-

pare ask students to think about their own thinking and to reflect on their contribution to and learning in the course. Students themselves are a resource for me as I ask questions and make judgments and decisions in grading and evaluation.

These structural aspects of classroom life are important at this time in my teaching. Changes will continue to come. Circle seating is the only aspect listed here that has been part of my teaching since I began in 1976. I describe the structural aspect of my Principia class to show the kind of context that supports response-centered practices. The list is not a prescription for all courses or all teachers.

PRIORITIES AND THE THINKING: TEACHER AND STUDENTS INTERPRET RESPONSE-CENTERED EXPERIENCES

The January 1993 Principia class provides the particular examples I use in telling this story of response-centered teaching and learning. At 8:30 A.M. three mornings a week, 25 Principia students and I climb four flights of stairs to see what response—what meanings and connections—students will make. The majority of readings and art/film texts for our interdisciplinary consideration of the theme "Freedom and Authority" come from the reading list designed by the Principia faculty. The selections, together with the students, shape this semester's Principia curriculum and are listed at the end of the chapter. Among our texts, the most notable diversions from the established reading list are those titles from or about Central America; and it seems to me that the story of how they came to be included illustrates principles of response.

In Principia, as in all of my courses, I aim to include one text that is a first-time reading experience for me. Only months earlier, as I was traveling in Central America with faculty peers (supported by a Global Studies grant through the college and the Knight Foundation), students at the public university in San Salvador urged me to read Salvadoran novelist Manlio Argueta's *One Day of Life* with my students. And so I met Principia students in January 1993 with anticipation. Here, at last, were the people with whom I would read Argueta's book. After talking about the novel, students wanted to continue our focus on Central American issues. In response to their request, we reworked our schedule and reading list. They asked to see the film *Romero* and continued to make unique, important connections among these views of life in contemporary El Salvador and works by Martin Luther King, Victor Frankl, Linda Hogan, Dostoevski, or Sophocles.

Making Connections

There are questions that help me reflect on the teaching and learning in my classroom, and they come along with me every time I meet with students. What do students have to say, what will they write, what images, stories, questions, and associations will come to mind for them in response to our readings and earlier conversations? I want to see their thinking and hear their meanings. One of the ways I think that this can happen is by asking students to continuously make connections between the pieces we read.

The work of shaping connections is, indeed, the work of constructing knowledge. For me, construction of knowledge is the aim of academic rigor. Shaping connections functions as an aim for each aspect of student thinking—reading, speaking, drawing, and writing. At the same time, these modes of thought function as processes toward the realization of ideas, connections, meanings, knowledge. There is wholeness: Aim and processes intertwine. There is support for development and continuation of ideas as well as for the exercise of fluid, flexible thought.

There is no right answer when the question is: What connections can you make? There are all kinds of possibilities to see, interpret, transform, imagine, compare and contrast, link, or question. Connecting takes a willingness to make leaps, from genre to genre, from discipline to discipline, from factual to fictional, and across cultures and eras. Connecting means finding focus. It culls meanings, sometimes distilling ideas to find points for intersection, sometimes elaborating toward that end. Connecting can mean creating a symbolic image, or naming a concept, or selecting a critical quotation, or forming a question that functions as the center—then bringing to it prior knowledge from previous texts or earlier conversation. While some of the possibilities turn out to be better than others, all of the connections make thinking visible.

Students and I continue to learn discernment. It is a surprisingly easy lesson. The better connections are immediately recognizable. They are better because they carry all of us further inside the texts and further inside our own thoughts and feelings. Better because they keep questions open or are genuinely memorable. Better because they suggest something of future possibilities by showing what more, what else might be discovered next time. Better because they slow us enough to think and feel, at the same time as they spur us on. Better because they teach us about human capacity for thought. At the close of the course, one student wrote about the work of making connections: "There are connections in so many things in this world that can be made and this class really brought that to light for me."

Looking back, I realize that it took some years for me to trust myself about putting the work of making connections as a top priority for Principia students. Doing so has changed some of my beliefs about students as readers and most of my classroom practice with regard to the use of student discussion groups. Though I knew making connections and finding meanings were the ways in which people learn, I had continued to let the academic rigor question bark loudly. My bias, from English, was for close textual readings. My first question was: Will students read closely if I do not make individual textual analysis our priority? Because this was my question, I thoughtfully prepared student discussion questions to guide groups toward explication of the text. Of course, the eight to ten questions I wrote for each text steered students toward the knowledge I valued most highly. Some of the questions directed students toward connections I had already, joyfully, made. Given those questions, try as they might, sometimes students didn't find the connections, or, if they did, their marveling over them was nothing like mine.

Only some years later did my question about student reading change. When moved long enough and deeply enough by the connections students were in fact making together in groups, after compliantly answering my prepared questions, I learned to ask: How are students reading in my course? The answer, in short, is this: They are reading and rereading where their questions are, where their meanings are, where they are awed. They are reading like readers, which is also to say they cut corners some of the time.

I learned to authentically notice students' reading, over time, by eavesdropping on student discussions toward the end of the 20 or 30 minutes allotted for my questions. At times groups addressed the list, then paused until I called them back to the full group. But at other times students started the work of authentically conversing about their reading in those few minutes after dealing with my handout of questions. And there it was: student response. Catching those smidgens of real conversation over the semester at last led me to a more authentic question about students as readers. Reflecting on my changed question has called me to look more widely at students' reading and their talk about the reading. It has called me deeper into trust.

The question I continue to ask about this particular semester in Principia is why so many students read so much and so well—so often. I continue to believe the answer is linked in part to my decision to make the work of making connections a top priority. It is linked as well to my aim that students respond by fully talking about what they read, rather than picking out answers for my questions. And so, Principia students come to class knowing they will do the talking. They come knowing they count on peers who, in turn, count on them to be ready for conversation. They come to class knowing that what they know, what they wonder about, what they discover, as readers and through talking and writing, is what the class is about. Early on winter mornings, Principia students come up the stairs to express what counts for them and ask the questions they need to ask of the texts, of me, of each other, and of themselves.

I believe Principia students are "reading without nonsense," Frank Smith's (1985) description of how readers read. Together, we are doing our best to establish a classroom context with natural reading purposes and patterns. Students are interested in what they themselves have to say. The classroom AH-HAS, I am convinced, are as moving for students witnessing a group presentation with beautiful connections as they are for those generating the particulars. There is a dynamic at work that seems part curiosity, part fellow-feeling, part impetus to take a turn at bringing all of us to the AH-HA point in recognition of authentic and meaningful work. I don't see traditional we'll-do-you-one-better or cut-throat competition between groups, though there clearly are bonds within the various small groups. In the end, the class is one group cooing over good ideas and stopping in our tracks when ideas, and the forms through which they are expressed, are breathtaking.

Individual Readers

As a class community we are, in the end, individual learners, working closely with peers, asking each other to keep questions open, and trusting ourselves to do "good works," Ken Macrorie's (1984) description of "what learners write, speak, or construct that counts for them, their fellow learners, their teachers, and persons outside the classroom" (p. xi).

Students read for Principia, I believe, in order to take part in the course—to enjoy working together, creating unique forms, and learning for themselves. At the close of the course, they write comments such as the following:

- Learning from each other is what is valuable. It is so much easier to develop thought processes when you can build on what someone in your group stated.
- Ideas flow in smaller groups. Then, it is neat that the ideas are spread into the big group.
- It [Principia] was taught differently so that you can learn for yourself.
- The reading gives me new thoughts and images of feelings; how I feel and how others feel. The talking helps to share what everyone is thinking. You get different ideas and different angles on the ideas you have.
- The reading and talking are very helpful to me. In small groups it is easy to talk about ideas and feelings because, since we have had the same group for so long, we have a kind of group community where anyone can feel free to contribute.
- Talking about the readings helps to make them more concrete in my mind. Having the same group helps all of us open up more and tell what we are really thinking.

Throughout the semester, I talk about reading assignments in ways that show I expect students to read for themselves—not for me. Instead of assigning a specific number of pages for the next class period, I ask well ahead of time that students try to be about a third of the way—or half-way, or finished—by a particular date. Readers set the pace for themselves. They don't need to put themselves on automatic pilot for 30 pages or three chapters the night before each class. What they need to do, throughout the semester, is read. Students write comments such as the following at the close of the course:

- The reading has been great and I'm glad that you give us enough time to read it (not one night).
- I really enjoyed the variety in our "assigned" reading. I place assigned within quotation marks because the reading assignments in this class were so enjoyable that I found myself consistently putting homework for my other classes off in order to read ahead—the assignments were hardly projects I had to force myself to complete "to get the grade" but rather were assignments that challenged me to really think. Often times

I would find myself wanting to reread the assigned material because I felt an idea (concept) was escaping me. When I did treat myself to a rereading and found that missing concept, I felt as if I had just discovered the missing link in an ancient puzzle that had been labeled "Unsolvable"—it was the greatest feeling!

Visual Response

With Principia students' responses central and the task of making connections among works and across disciplines a top priority, I make a further commitment to explore the potential of visual imagery in meaning-making. Clearly, all response-centered activities do not involve visuals. But from what I had seen in previous sections of Principia and teacher education classes, the invitation to use visual images, symbols, designs, and patterns, both as tools for reaching ideas and as expressions of well-formed ideas, holds student interest.

Initially, I viewed the commitment to visual expression as a matter of pedagogy. Working together to create visuals is as much at the heart of how students and I come together as is conversation and writing. What comes to surprise me, and students as well, is how thoroughly our use of visual expression becomes a matter of curriculum. I believe it to be because we approach visual meaning-making consistently rather than as a one-time or fun-time strategy.

Reading print and nonprint texts (film and art), writing, talking and listening, and creating visual imagery are our work. This semester, I ask students to value visual expression equally with speech and writing as processes that can move us toward "release of meaning" (Greene, 1979, p. 123). We look at the content of visuals in order to see thinking. What we find is essential human thought. It is intellectual and emotive. It is symbolic, metaphorical, ironic, perhaps either exaggerated or simplified, perhaps generalized or particularized, associative, patterned (which is to say clearly organized or chaotic by design). The content of the visuals students create, just as the content of their conversation and writing, reenters the course as curriculum. It calls out further response, reappearing as more connections are formed and transforming as students' medium of expression changes. At one point a collaboratively created visual image functions as an outline for the formal essays written by five individual students.

I suggest two forms for students' visual responses. Groups create

what we call response-centered posters, and individuals work with
a rendition of what Gabriela Rico (1991a) describes as "one-pagers."
For collaborative visuals, I provide large sheets of newsprint and ask
students to bring sets of colored markers. My directions are, from
the beginning, slim:

> Please represent your conversation. You may draw images, or
> designs, or symbols, or patterns. You may use words. Quotations
> from the readings might work for you. Use whatever you need
> to represent your conversation. It doesn't matter how well you
> draw. We'll get the idea with stick-drawings!

And because it is a top priority this semester, I remind students to
see what connections can be made.

One-pagers, as Principia students and I use them, are individual
visual responses created on sheets of unlined typing paper. They
include an image, design, symbol, or pattern; at least two quotes
from the reading; and both a question and a statement from the student. Since I ask students to continuously make connections, the
one-pagers often include quotes from previous readings or questions
and statements that make leaps. Figures 7.1 and 7.2 are reproductions of student one-pagers (originally created using pens or pencils
and colored markers). I ask for a collaborative visual representing
group conversations every day, a request I sometimes question on
days when one-pagers are also being created. But students are creative in ways I haven't anticipated. One-pagers become resources,
intellectually and literally, for paper collages.

The guidelines I offer for group response-centered posters and
individual one-pagers are, by my own and students' experience,
minimal. I believe invitations for authentic student response need
to be bare-bones. After only a few class meetings, I no longer offer
even minimal directions. Groups gather and move to their work
spaces. Student study groups spend about 50 minutes of our 70-
minute class period together.

Sometimes I make my own visual while students work. I make
walking tours, stopping briefly with each group two or three times
in the hour. The questions students asked me in the past, about how
long a writing should be, or when an assignment is due, or if a particular thesis sentence is OK to use, aren't the kinds of questions I
now hear. If a group has remarkably varying understandings of a
symbol or passage, I am asked what I think. Students ask me historical and contextual questions. If someone has read a piece that con-

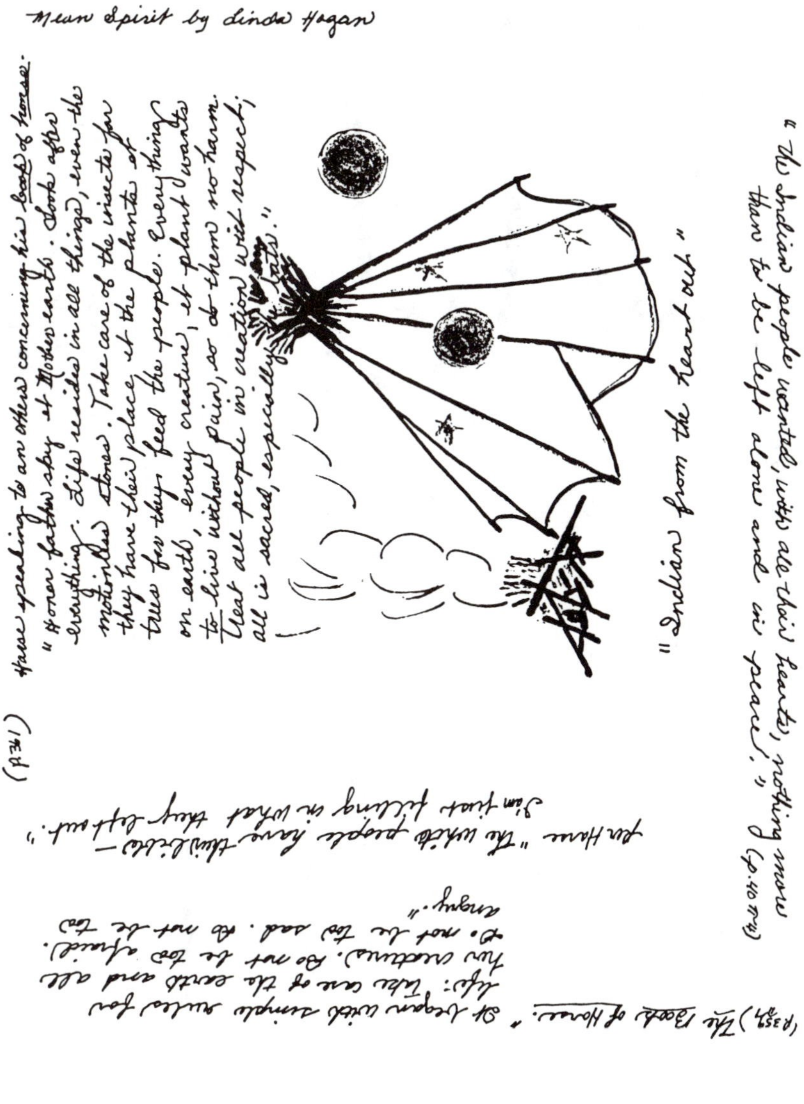

Figure 7.1. One-pager (Rico, 1991) by Rita S. Adams.

Figure 7.2. One-pager (Rico, 1991) by Gretchen Rud.

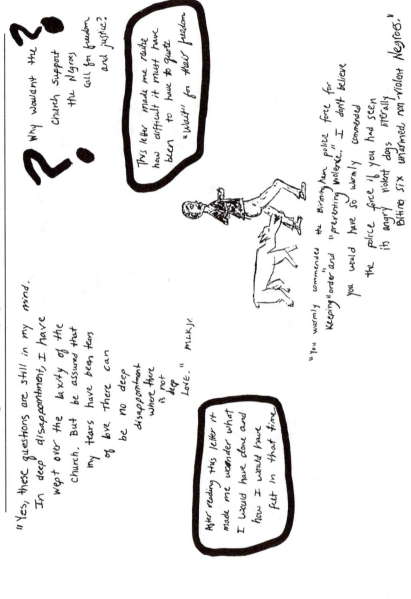

nects and remembers essential details or perhaps a quotation but can't recall the title or author, I am asked.

Near the close of the period the full class reunites to see the various response posters, hear brief explications and interpretations of the visuals, and visit about the work or issues raised. From the first day, students set the standard themselves, seeing what has been done and moving forward. I listen and applaud. And silently cheer my own greatest stride—trust.

The end-of-term self-evaluation questions I ask students to consider are specific. I ask what I want to know: "Tell me what you can about how you come up with an image for your one-pager, how you know which quotes are important to include with visuals, and where your questions come from." Students respond with comments such as the following:

- I learned a lot by putting ideas down through mapping with images and words and not just through paper [written] form. I loved the way you let us choose our own individual methods of express.
- The questions that I ask in my one-pagers are usually questions I have asked myself while I was reading. The image is what I think of the most when I start my one-pager—it is usually something that reminds me of what I have read.
- The image I use on my one-pagers comes from the symbol I think is most important in the story. My questions usually come from when I'm reading the story or writing about it. I use the quotes that stand out to me and symbolize something.
- Usually ideas or words stay with me after reading and I try to remember them and find them in the material for quotes or a picture. I pertain my questions to how something can be changed or why something needs to be changed.
- I use the quotes that had stood out the most while reading. I base my questions on what the most basic themes were. I take into account all the ideas suggested in a reading and try to come up with a main idea to relate through a picture.
- Certain images "pop" into my head when I read a book or watch a movie. These images are easily put on paper because I am an art minor. The quotes I choose are the ones that have the most impact on the image. The quote is part of the book or movie that sticks in your head word-for-word.
- Usually the image I use is a kind of picture of either some-

thing that has great importance in the book or a scene that is especially powerful—sometimes I think of symbolic-type things, but usually I just use main themes to help. When I read, certain parts strike me as true or relevant and I use them to find quotes. The questions I write just come when I think about the theme and subject of the reading. Other people contribute to my work through discussion.

• For images, I try and pick one that best represents a major point in the book/poem, whatever. Or maybe something that may seem small but really isn't. As for the quotes, I'm not sure how I know they are important. They just kind of come to you. The questions seem to be the easiest to come up with because it's just what you think could/should be answered.

The meanings students make are their own, and they take visual response in their own directions as well. The first time a group asks for tape and turns a poster into a construction, I know they have claimed not only their ideas but their forms of expression. As Figure 7.3 shows, students tear, fold, tape, and collage their way to further meanings and connections.

Written Response

Because students trust that what I want to know is what they themselves think and how they respond, they extend and vary each form of expression I suggest. Just as they add constructions and collages to their repertoire when working with visuals, they find ways to elaborate their writing. For the first time in my experience teaching Principia, some students write formal essays that make use of extended metaphor. They, of course, use metaphorical language. But they also depend on metaphor, reached through visual imagery, as an organizational structure. Figure 7.4 shows a group poster that later functioned as the central organizing device—an outline—for the essay writing at least three group members chose to do. In this case, the visual image physically shapes the metaphor, thereby suggesting linguistic imagery. It further shapes thought by providing an organizational pattern for the written pieces.

Some students prepare formal illustrations to accompany essays. Some write poetry and letters, carefully including specific quotations from the readings and shaping connections, as these are the

Figure 7.3. Group response-poster made in response to *Romero* (Languin, 1989) with connections to earlier selections.

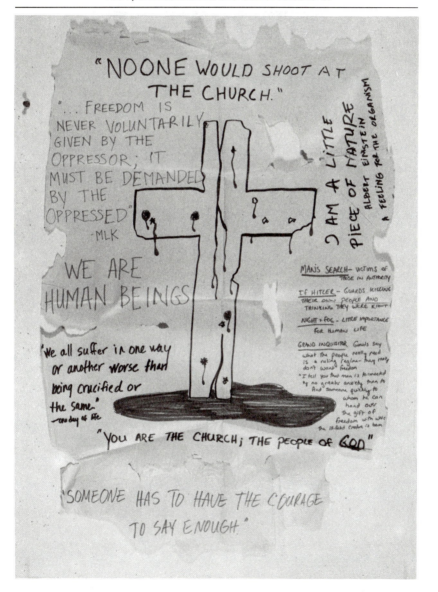

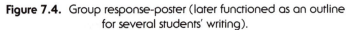

Figure 7.4. Group response-poster (later functioned as an outline for several students' writing).

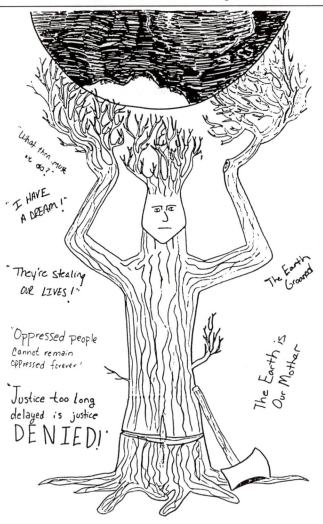

two requests I make of them as writers. At the close of the semester, students make comments such as these:

- I really enjoyed using the image which developed in our group as the basis for my paper. It really helped to draw things together.
- I felt good about the writing we did. I have always been able to put ideas together with words, but the idea of linking all these different stories [texts] to each other through a common theme [thesis] was fascinating.
- The writing, to me, was one of the best parts of the course. I thought it was great how the assignments were so open and the choices were left up to us. I think ideas come much easier when you're not worried about guidelines.
- I liked the idea that we could use images and unique forms to write our papers. The paper was easy to write. I was so interested with it and once I found the idea to connect my ideas together, it just seemed to flow.
- I didn't really think about it then but when we were doing those one-pagers, somebody wrote a quote on them and I thought that would be a good topic so I kind of took her idea but she wasn't going to use it so I didn't think it was too big a deal. I asked her and she said fine.
- I was glad that there weren't any guidelines because then it really gets your mind working to find exactly what you are going to write about. It helped to see the ideas you thought would work. [I offer suggestions if students ask me to help them weigh potential ideas.] But I think most of the topics came from within group discussion or looking at the posters or at least that's where mine came from.
- I thought this paper was great. I was allowed to be creative and express myself through methods other than summary response.
- Deep thinking, due to the readings, provided the means for making the writings "easier." I enjoy this class—my needs are met.
- I liked that these were papers you could write about anything you wanted. It is easier to write about something you want to and have picked to write on. I think it went well. I wrote on racism because it is the most interesting to me. It was scary at first to think that you had really no guidelines. It was kind of like where do I start? Then I picked a topic and it went really well. I liked it better this way rather than having guidelines.

REFLECTIONS FROM MY TEACHING JOURNAL

Using response-centered approaches, in liberal arts and secondary teacher education courses, I am as full of questions as of confidence. Most of the time, these days, I feel beside the point in my classroom. That is exactly how I now believe I should feel. I am needed to structure, prioritize, guide, and encourage maintenance of community, support students' thinking, provide information when students ask or when misinformation creates incorrect conclusions

I keep a journal about my teaching to reflect on the changes in my questions, beliefs, and practices. Journal freewritings allow me to describe and narrate classroom life. In this entry, I both describe and reflect on Principia students' thinking:

> As a central image on the first day of conversation about *One Day of Life* one group draws the wreckage of a bombed bus, another draws the badly beaten face of a man. I see and feel these images still.
>
> The image of the bus fills the poster. Bodies of the dead and pools of blood spilled from the bus. From broken windows, jagged blue lines cut the air. Smoke and flames and crumpled metal. I walk by the group and say, "This is what it feels like to be in El Salvador. You have an image here that expresses exactly what I felt in San Salvador." The image speaks shattering, spilling, fear.
>
> Another group creates an image of Chepe's face [see Figure 7.5]. Lupe, a grandmother who has lost Chepe, her husband, and many family members in the Salvadoran repression, narrates the novel. Now, she fears for the life of her granddaughter. She relives the day the Guard brings Chepe through the streets, asking if anyone can identify him. Lupe recognizes his clothing but not his beaten face. She keeps a promise made to Chepe that, even if asked to identify him, she will protect herself and family by denying him. I don't know him, she tells the Guard, how could anyone know such a disfigured man? In that moment Chepe opens his remaining eye. As if to say good-bye, Lupe thinks, or maybe as a thank you for keeping the promise. The group's image covers the page. Quotations from the novel tell of the pointlessness of violence and name the fear that swells in the hearts of people subjected to continuing terror.
>
> We watch *Romero* [a full-length film depicting the life of Archbishop Oscar Romero]. The closing footage shows black and

Figure 7.5. Group response-poster made in response to *One Day of Life* (Argueta, 1991) with connections to earlier selections.

Figure 7.6. Group response-poster made in response to *Romero* (Languin, 1989) with visual imagery shaping metaphorical connections to earlier selections, specifically *Mean Spirit* (Hogan, 1990).

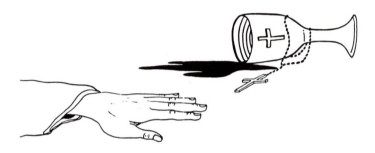

"Praise the Lord, and pass the ammunition."

white photographs of torture victims from San Salvador. The images peel past one by one. Then there it is: an actual photograph of a head and face, shaped and torn like the image of Chepe students created. The image came for us, first, through a novelist's written imagery. Next, from students' interpretation and rendering. Finally, a film director's choice to mix cinema and photographic record of the aftermath of terror, confirms the visual image.

I am fascinated by the connections students make between works when we talk about their posters. A good example comes from the image of wine/blood spilled from a communion challis, part of a group's response to *Romero* [see Figure 7.6]. We talk about how the image invites interpretation, suggesting both wine and blood. We talk about the motion the image holds, as if a bird in flight. At that moment the image reminds us of the symbolic importance of bats and the bat-cave in Linda Hogan's *Mean Spirit*. That opens conversation connecting the role of the church in Salvador's repression with issues of Indian spirituality during the oppression of Oklahoma Indians.

Journal writing, for me, is a vehicle for expressing my appreciation of student work. Their work interests and amazes me. I focus on student thinking and ask myself how it is that their thinking is made visible—made available, made knowable—to themselves, to their peers, to me.

It is the actual work—the actual thinking—that actual students do in response-centered classrooms that barks back at the neighbor's dog. The rigor is in the thinking. When literacy experiences invite authentic expression, real students do really rigorous work. It is work I see as skillful and scholarly, creative, integrative, analytical, questioning, and reflective. It is work that sometimes stands alone and sometimes leads to whole new areas for inquiry. It is thinking that holds voice and releases students' meanings. If academic rigor means knowing what the teacher knows, well, then that's a bear growling somewhere outside of my neighborhood.

PRINCIPIA SELECTIONS: FREEDOM AND AUTHORITY

Autobiography

Frankl, Victor. (1984). *Man's search for meaning: An introduction to logotherapy* (I. Lasch, Trans.). New York: Touchstone/Simon & Schuster. (Original work published 1959)

Art

Kollwitz, Hans. (Ed.). (1988). *The diary and letters of Kaethe Kollwitz* (R. & C. Winston, Trans.). Evanston, IL: Northwestern University Press.
Kollwitz, Kaethe. Slide reproductions of artwork, including lithos, woodcuts, posters, and sculpture.

Biography

Keller, Evelyn Fox, & Freeman, W. H. (1983). *A feeling for the organism: The life and work of Barbara McClintock.* New York: Freeman.

Classics

Dostoevski, Fyodor. (1948). *The grand inquisitor on the nature of man* (C. Garnett, Trans.). New York: Macmillan. (Original work published 1880)
Exodus. (1977). In *The new Oxford annotated Bible.* New York: Oxford University Press.
Plato. (1981). Apology. In G. M. A. Grube (Trans.), *Plato: Five dialogues* (pp. 23–44). Indianapolis, IN: Hackett.

Plato. (1981). Crito. In G. M. A. Grube (Trans.), *Plato: Five dialogues* (pp. 45–56). Indianapolis, IN: Hackett.

Sophocles. (1960). Antigone. In P. D. Arnott (Ed. & Trans.), *Oedipus the king and Antigone* (pp. 1–56). Arlington Heights, IL: Harlan Davidson.

Essays and Letters

King, Martin Luther, Jr. (1986). Letter from Birmingham city jail. In J. M. Washington (Ed.), *A testament of hope: The essential writings and speeches of Martin Luther King, Jr.* (pp. 289–302). New York: HarperCollins.

Meyer, Philip. (1970, February). If Hitler asked you to electrocute a stranger, would you? *Esquire*, pp. 73, 128, 130, 132.

Sanger, Margaret. (1973). Birth control—A parents' problem or woman's? In A. Rossi (Ed.), *The feminist papers: From Adams to de Beauvior* (pp. 533–536). New York: Bantam. (Original work published 1920)

Staples, Brent. (1993). Black men and public space. In J. Madden & S. M. Blake (Eds.), *Emerging voices: Readings in the American experience* (2nd ed.; pp. 440–442). New York: Harcourt Brace Jovanovich.

Fiction

Argueta, Manlio. (1991). *One day of life* (B. Brow, Trans.). New York: Random House. (Original work published 1980)

Chopin, Kate. (1969). The story of an hour. In *Complete works of Kate Chopin* (pp. 352–354). Baton Rouge: Louisiana State University Press. (Original work published 1894)

Hogan, Linda. (1990). *Mean spirit.* New York: Atheneum.

Films

Languin, John. (Director). (1989). *Romero* [Film]. Santa Monica, CA: Vidmark Entertainment.

Resnais, Alain. (Director). (1955). *Night and fog* [Film]. Chicago, IL: Films Inc. Video.

Weir, Peter. (Director). (1982). *The year of living dangerously* [Film]. Los Angeles: MGM/UA Entertainment, WEA Corporation.

CHAPTER 8

We Travel Together in Circles: Processes and Themes from Our Stories of Response-Centered Teaching and Teacher Research

KARLA SMART

Story moves. Narrative journeys through time and across settings and perspectives. It travels through changes in characters' lives and beliefs. It moves through the complexities and ironies of plot. At times it may appear as though nothing wiggles, neither questions nor resolutions, reason nor emotion. But narrative winds, despite impediments. It cuts paths or returns to known trails. The telling or writing of story renders images and symbols, themes, patterns of voice, issues, and questions along the way. Ultimately, listeners, readers, and writers travel together. Their movement is a stretch toward understanding, an embrace of perspectives and possibilities, a construction of meaning and truths, a journey of learning.

We six teacher-researchers, writers of *Stories from Response-Centered Classrooms,* recognize the movement of story. We live, teach, and write a story of educational beliefs and teaching practice. Janice calls our work a journey. Teresa knows we move with courage. Our real lives, and the real lives of students, their families, our colleagues and administrators, texture the narrative. Teresa writes of our inquiry:

> We have traveled together in circles, questioning one another, trying out new ideas and sharing complex problems, celebrating new discoveries about the learning process. This takes great courage. Each of us has stepped out of a deceivingly comfortable

pattern of relating to students and "sharing" knowledge with students, and has attempted to allow learning to become a more natural process.

OUR RESPONSE-CENTERED TEACHING PROCESSES BECOME APPROACHES TO QUALITATIVE TEACHER RESEARCH

Paulo Freire attributes to Spanish poet Antonio Machado the proverb "se hace camino al andar." Freire uses its wisdom to describe the motion of education and social change: "I think that even though we need to have some outline, *I am sure that we make the road by walking*" (Horton & Freire, 1990, p. 6). We six colleagues recognize ourselves as journeying road-makers. Carrying with us "outlines" from the past, we have moved with the stories of our response-centered classrooms. Our process of inquiry itself is a story. Deb credits our growth, from the beginning, to how we chose to move, "building through the process students [were] asked to use" in response-centered classrooms. Many ideas, questions, and themes connect or extend various paths we have cut as teachers and as researchers in this work.

This chapter closes our text but not our work. The elements that, today, form and make whole the text of *Stories from Response-Centered Classrooms* remain in motion for us. We continue to move the images, questions, and perspectives, considering the themes and patterns that form. We continue to walk and talk our stories of response-centered teaching, reflecting on particular students and classroom patterns from the past, considering the needs and issues of current school people in our lives, and planning for opportunities and students as yet unmet. Readers of our stories, we know, also walk journeys of learning; their response will be the questions, connections, and meanings that move their own spoken or written, formal or informal narratives. Their responses hold potential for further inquiry.

Naming themes has been a natural part of conversation all along. A question particularly useful to us throughout our work is: What is of essence in our stories of response-centered teaching? Over the years we told what stood out to us in our own teaching story, in all of our stories together, and through our processes for collaborative inquiry. Talk would slip back and forth between theoretical beliefs and teaching practices. We would describe experience and think together about it. We would reflect, interpret, make connections to theory, question and elaborate on ideas. From the beginning, a second question was also important to us: What further implications, questions, and possibilities, given our theoretical beliefs and stories of response-centered teaching, come to mind?

Notes in my teaching journal, written 6 months into our collaboration and years before we imagined writing together for publication, suggest headings for themes that travel through our stories of response-centered teaching. Reading the notes, I recognize each of us individually and all of us together. Yet each life and story of teaching has changed. Our personal lives and professional lives mesh. Since coming together as colleagues, we have seen marriages, a divorce, degree completions, new teaching positions, promotions and tenures, and professional disappointments as well as accomplishments. Commitment to response-centered teaching and teacher research remains. Change, it seems to me, has had to do with understanding ourselves as scholars and the intensity we bring to our work; with our sense of urgency in finding and creating supportive, educative relationships with colleagues; and with our deepening understandings of both doubt and fluidity in classroom life. Deb uses freewriting to trace layers in her journey:

> Learning to teach the way I want to live; learning how I want to live and teach. Discovering who students are, how they learn; discovering who I am as a teacher because of who I was as a student because of who I am as a person, because of who my teachers were, [and] how and what they taught me and/or didn't teach me. This group's process has allowed me to develop the way I hope my own students can develop: I created knowledge based on my prior knowledge—"theory of the world in the head" [Smith, 1985]—and new ideas presented in the context of conversations with authors (Smith, Purves, Cusick, etc.) through reading, and conversations within our group as we compared our theories and responses. All this took place within the supportive framework of caring people who listened, affirmed, and responded—helping me shape and reshape ideas and beliefs which have become a central, sturdy, steady foundation on which I've built—more truly, *am building*—the teaching approaches I use in my classroom.

THEMES AND MEANINGS

The possibilities for thematizing and discussing meaning do not end with the closing chapter of *Stories from Response-Centered Class-*

rooms. The themes and issues that stand out to us continue to hold our interest; we as teacher-researchers benefit when our questions remain vital and we continue to seek out lively conversations. Education, in general, benefits as well. One reader of an early draft of our manuscript suggested that our stories were about more than we claimed. The layering and connecting of ideas our work includes, it seems to us, invite readers' responses. We have not aimed to claim a last word; the themes that follow are broadly stated.

Early in our work the headings we used were full-circle quality, relationship, trust, and fullness of ideas/responses. Patterns became visible. We observed recurring ideas or questions in the details of our stories, then named and grouped them. Over time, we reached further themes as particular words and ideas became motifs for us as individuals and thematic concepts for us as colleagues. We continue to celebrate language together: Janice's gift of the idea of "resonance," Teresa's thoughtful elaboration on "authenticity," Joyce's understanding of "complexity," my own insistence on "trust," Deb's ever-deepening understandings of "respect," and Barb's careful yet expansive considerations of "knowledge" and "learning." Thinking about and living what these ideas mean to us, in the light of response-centered teaching, has taken time and nurtured change.

Our stories are about wholeness. We see how much of a piece our work is. Its full-circle quality presents itself through the idea of change. We began together, envisioning a need to change. Theory, all along, has been foundational. But through the processes we used in response-centered teaching and collaborative research, we moved deeper into theory. That move means tc us that theory truly is a tool for expanding our visions of classroom practice. We have desire, and energy, and ideas to help us move toward change.

Our work is about relationship. The processes of inquiry unfold a story of collegial relationship. Response-centered teaching invites authentic and full teacher–student, as well as student–student, relationships. Response-centered teaching develops out of thinking respectfully about students as thinkers. It creates ways of being together with students, and of students being together with peers, that invite students' ideas and welcome their preferences for expression. There is potential for change in relationship for everyone: teacher to student, student to teacher, student to self, student to peers, teacher to self, and teacher to peers.

Our stories of response-centered teaching and teacher research are about trust. The processes moving in our work allow teachers to trust themselves as resources, to trust students as knowledgeable and to see their work as creation of meaning. Response-centered teaching is about freeing teachers and students to trust themselves. All are welcome to claim preferred patterns of response, and all are afforded opportunities to explore cognitive and emotional ranges through work with unfamiliar mediums and processes. Teachers and students learn and try new tools for exercise of imagination, reflection, questioning, organization, and expression. Response-centered teaching nurtures trust by trusting people to be responsible, authentic, knowledgeable beings.

Our stories are about the fullness of human response, seen in the expressions of teachers, learners, researchers. Authentic response is fully human. It holds creativity, reason, emotion, pattern, and wonder. Response-centered classrooms offer people the fullness of their own responses, their own humanity. Students and teachers are freed to have their work honored. Response-centered teaching invites them to *be* and to *grow*. It invites them to question—and to recognize and leave open those questions of meaning that life will not allow us to close. Response-centered teaching is very different from the reductive, the technocratic, the judgmental, and the silencing in education.

Our work is about the discovery of recurring questions, thematic questions. It asks, in Deb's words, "What is important knowledge?" Because response-centered teaching seeks authentic reflection and appropriate, useful evaluation, Barb suggests: "The real question should be what have students learned rather than what have they learned that we planned for them to learn." Our work asks questions about the expression and understanding of responses. We wonder about the nature of communication with school people, in all roles, and with parents and the public. We know, for example, that colleagues and parents holding behaviorist views of learning, or those placing high value on standardized tests, ask different questions and attribute different meanings to language and theory about students and teachers, about teaching, and about learning.

The range of themes we have come to know through our stories of response-centered teaching reflects, in Joyce's words, "the complexities of issues and facets of teaching: curriculum, methods, purpose, philosophy, student personalities, classroom organization, evaluation." Teachers and students, together as the class community, must live with and imagine new possibilities in light of complexities and even paradox.

Our stories are about ideal visions and actual realities, and about the inconsistencies that stretch between the two realms. The concept of community provides an example. Thomas Moore understands that paradox is part of community, which is soulfully part of relationships of learning. Moore (1994) writes:

> Much of my work is based on the insights, imagery, and worldview of the Florentine Academy headed by Marsilio Ficino in the later decades of the fifteenth century. Scholars debate about the nature of the structure of this academy, but for Ficino himself it was clearly not a simple institute of teaching, but a living community of friends. . . . Community is born when individual and group are no longer felt to be two independent realities. Like all soul entities, community is a paradox. (pp. 91, 106)

Our stories of response-centered teaching trace the importance of friendships to community (Cusick, 1973) and the importance of community to authentic learning. Yet paradox is visible in our classrooms. Teresa writes about the community she and students share:

> I know that my classroom has yet to transform into the ideal community of learners where curiosities are piqued, where each feels safe in exploring and sharing, where there is full equality in respectful relationships. Sometimes the learning occurs behind my back, when I'm not checking for understanding, not looking for results. That's the way it should be. My greatest reward is to observe the evolution of readers, writers, and responders.

Janice, too, writes about an ideal context for response-centered class communities and the learning journeys that are made there:

> People who feel secure in their environment, who know that those around them respect and value them, and who are confident in their own abilities, will journey far. A response-centered approach to learning affirms students as capable human beings who will have the courage to be among the risk-takers and curious who ask difficult questions and arrive at important answers. If learning is a journey, this approach helps make it a safer, more secure one.

INVITATION

We travel in circles and live with layers of complexity. The themes this chapter briefly describes connect powerfully to each other.

Wholeness, of course, is a visible aspect of full human response. And trust is critical to relationship. Each of these ideas contributes to how we think about and experience community, how we think about and practice teaching.

Response-centered teaching, for us six teacher colleagues, is about reflecting on beliefs and values, experiencing process, listening for and expressing authentic meanings, and making friends with change. Knowledge created through the movement of narrative has given us rich material for building roads. The process, patterns, and themes central to our stories of teaching function, as well, in our story of collaborative qualitative teacher research. Intersections exist along the road, and there is potential creative construction of many more. Questions remain, and further questions remain to be imagined. We look to colleagues and students, from a range of disciplines, to join the journey.

References

Atwell, N. (1987). *In the middle: Writing, reading, and learning with adolescents.* Portsmouth, NH: Boynton/Cook.

Barnes, D. (1992). *From communication to curriculum* (2nd ed.). Portsmouth, NH: Boynton/Cook.

Benton, M., & Fox, G. (1985). *Teaching literature nine to fourteen.* Oxford: Oxford University Press.

Boomer, G. (1987). Addressing the problem of elsewhereness: A case for action research in schools. In D. Goswami & P. Stillman (Eds.), *Reclaiming the classroom: Teacher research as an agency for change* (pp. 4–13). Upper Montclair, NJ: Boynton/Cook.

Britton, J. (1970). *Language and learning.* London: Penguin.

Bruner, J. (1986). *Actual minds, possible worlds.* Cambridge, MA: Harvard University Press.

Carlsen, G. R., & Sherrill, A. (1988). *Voices of readers: How we come to love books.* Urbana, IL: National Council of Teachers of English.

Cusick, P. (1973). *Inside high school: The student's world.* New York: Holt, Rinehart & Winston.

Dewey, J. (1934). *Art as experience.* New York: Minton, Balch.

Dewey, J. (1944). *Democracy and education.* New York: Free Press. (Original work published 1916)

Edwards, A., & Westgate, D. (1987). *Investigating classroom talk.* London: Falmer.

Elbow, P. (1973). *Writing without teachers.* London: Oxford University Press.

Elbow, P. (1981). *Writing with power: Techniques for mastering the writing process.* New York: Oxford University Press.

Emig, J. (1977). Writing as a mode of learning. *College Composition and Communication, 28,* 122–128.

Fox, M. (1993). *Radical reflections: Passionate opinions on teaching, learning, and living.* San Diego: Harcourt Brace.

Freire, P. (1970). *Pedagogy of the oppressed* (M. B. Ramos, Trans.). New York: Continuum.

Freire, P. (1994). *Pedagogy of hope: Reliving pedagogy of the oppressed* (R. R. Barr, Trans.). New York: Continuum. (Original work published 1992)

Fulwiler, T. (1982). Writing: An act of cognition. In C. W. Griffin (Ed.), *New directions for teaching and learning: Teaching writing in all disciplines.* San Francisco: Jossey-Bass.

Greene, M. (1978). *Landscapes of learning.* New York: Teachers College Press.

Greene, M. (1979). Language, literature, and the release of meaning. *College English, 41*(2), 123–135.

Greene, M. (1982). Literacy for what? *Phi Delta Kappan, 63*(5), 326–329.

Greene, M. (1988). *The dialectic of freedom.* New York: Teachers College Press.

Halliday, M. (1978). *Language as social semiotic: The social interpretations of language and meaning.* London: Edward Arnold.

Harste, J., Woodward, V., & Burke, C. (1984). *Language stories and literacy lessons.* Portsmouth, NH: Heinemann.

Horton, M., & Freire, P. (1990). *We make the road by walking: Conversations on education and social change* (B. Bell, J. Gaventa, & J. Peters, Eds.). Philadelphia: Temple University Press.

Kirby, D., & Kuykendall, C. (1991). *Mind matters: Teaching for thinking.* Portsmouth, NH: Boynton/Cook.

Langer, J. (1992). *Literature instruction: A focus on student response.* Urbana, IL: National Council of Teachers of English.

Livdahl, B. S. (1993). To read it is to live it, different from just knowing it. *Journal of Reading, 37*(3), 192–200.

Lloyd-Jones, R., & Lunsford, A. (1989). *The English coalition conference: Democracy through language.* Urbana, IL: National Council of Teachers of English.

Macrorie, K. (1970). *Uptaught.* Rochelle Park, NJ: Hayden.

Macrorie, K. (1974). *A vulnerable teacher.* Rochelle Park, NJ: Hayden.

Macrorie, K. (1980). *Searching writing: A contextbook.* Rochelle Park, NJ: Hayden.

Macrorie, K. (1984). *Twenty teachers.* New York: Oxford University Press.

Macrorie, K. (1985). *Telling writing* (4th ed.). Portsmouth, NH: Boynton/Cook.

Marshall, J. D. (1988). Introduction. Two ways of knowing: Relations between research and practice in the teaching of writing. In J. S. Davis & J. D. Marshall (Eds.), *Ways of knowing: Research and practice in the teaching of writing* (pp. 1–14). Iowa City, IA: Iowa Council of Teachers of English.

Martin, N. (1988). Introduction. In M. Lightfoot & N. Martin (Eds.), *The word for teaching is learning: Essays for James Britton* (pp. ix–xvii). London: Heinemann.

Moffett, J. (1979). Integrity in the teaching of writing. *Phi Delta Kappan, 61*, 276–279.

Moffett, J. (1983). Reading and writing as meditation. *Language Arts, 60*, 315–332.

Moore, T. (1994). *Soul mates: Honoring the mysteries of love and relationship.* New York: HarperCollins.

Murray, D. (1985). *A writer teaches writing* (2nd ed.). Boston: Houghton Mifflin.

Pradl, G. (1988). Learning listening. In M. Lightfoot & N. Martin (Eds.), *The word for teaching is learning: Essays for James Britton* (pp. 38–48). London: Heinemann.

Probst, R. W. (1988). Readers and literary texts. In B. F. Nelms (Ed.), *Literature in the classroom: Readers, texts, and contexts* (pp. 19–29). New York: Longman.

Purves, A., Rogers, T., & Soter, A (1990). *How porcupines make love II: Teaching a response-centered literature curriculum.* New York: Longman.

Rico, G. L. (1983). *Writing the natural way.* Los Angeles: Tarcher.

Rico, G. L. (1991a). Conference on English leadership brunch. National Council of Teachers of English fall conference, Seattle, WA.

Rico, G. L. (1991b). *Pain and possibility: Writing your way through personal crisis.* Los Angeles: Tarcher.

Rief, L. (1992). *Seeking diversity: Language arts with adolescents.* Portsmouth, NH: Boynton/Cook.

Romano, T. (1987). *Clearing the way: Working with teenage writers.* Portsmouth, NH: Boynton/Cook.

Rosenblatt, L. (1978). *The reader, the text, the poem: The transactional theory of the literary work.* Carbondale: Southern Illinois University Press.

Smith, F. (1985). *Reading without nonsense* (2nd ed.). New York: Teachers College Press.

Traugh, C. (1985). Computers: A reflection. In S. Harlow (Ed.), *Humanistic perspectives on computers in the schools* (pp. 85–94). New York: Haworth.

Vygotsky, L. (1978). *Mind in society: The development of higher psychological processes.* Cambridge, MA: Harvard University Press.

About the Authors

Janice L. Anderson teaches at Ben Franklin Junior High School in Fargo, North Dakota. She has taught for many years in a variety of positions, including preschool to adult education, gifted and talented education, and reading. Currently she teaches seventh- and eighth-grade English on an interdisciplinary team in her school. A graduate of North Dakota State University in Fargo, she continues to do graduate work in her field. She has made presentations at the Concordia Reading Conference, Concordia College, Moorhead, Minnesota, and at the National Council of Teachers of English convention in Seattle, Washington, in 1991.

Debra Kramer Geiger has taught secondary-level English for four years in Minnesota public schools. She is an active member of the National Council of Teachers of English, the Minnesota Council of Teachers of English, and the Minnesota Writing Project. She has been a presenter at the 1991 National Council of Teachers of English Convention, the 1993 Fall Convention of the Minnesota Council of Teachers of English, and co-directed two seasons of the Young Writer's Workshop, a workshop-style writing minicourse for middle school students of diverse cultural and community backgrounds in the Twin Cities area offered by the Minnesota Writing Project. Deb earned her bachelor's degree in English from Concordia College in Moorhead, Minnesota, and is currently pursuing a graduate degree in English.

Teresa Krinke Herbert is a graduate of Concordia College in Moorhead, Minnesota, and she teaches at Minnetonka Middle School–East in Minnetonka, Minnesota. A member of a local Teacher Applying Whole Language (TAWL) group, she has made presentations with colleagues at two Minnesota TAWL fall conferences. Currently she is working toward her masters of education degree at the University of Minnesota in Minneapolis.

Barbara Smith Livdahl is an associate professor of education and chair of the education department at Valparaiso University, Valparaiso, Indiana. In this position she teaches undergraduate and graduate courses in content reading, qualitative teacher research, and educational assessment and evaluation. During her more than 20 years in public and private secondary schools, she has taught English, German, reading, and special education math and language arts; she has also served as a coordinator of special education and reading. She completed a portion of her doctoral work in Oxford, England, where she studied the use of oral and written language for learning. She earned her Ed.D. from the University of North Dakota in 1991. Because she is convinced that the response-centered approach offers the best hope for educating America's future workers and citizens, she continues to study ways to increase the understanding and commitment of both preservice and inservice teachers to these new ways of thinking, learning, and teaching.

Karla Smart is associate professor of education and English at Concordia College, Moorhead, Minnesota. She earned her Ph.D. from the University of North Dakota in 1985, where her focus was secondary literacy education. She has been a high school teacher of English and a junior college writing instructor; presently she is an educator in secondary teacher education and liberal arts courses. She has worked as Writer in Residence in public schools, sponsored by the North Dakota Council on the Arts. She worked as a poet in a faculty/student writers and artists collaborative study of landscape and creative processes. She is currently studying literature and pedagogy from Central America, where she has traveled with an interdisciplinary team of faculty interested in the political, cultural, and pedagogical contributions of people engaged in the struggle for literacy, voice, and power.

Joyce Wallman teaches ninth-grade English at Ben Franklin Junior High in Fargo, North Dakota. She is a 1995 recipient of a National Endowment for the Humanities grant for the study of literature of the Holocaust. She has 17 years of teaching experience in both public and private schools, grades 7–12. She is professionally active on many district committees and has been a presenter at the Concordia Reading Conference, the North Dakota Education Association convention, and the 1991 National Council of Teachers of English convention. She completed her undergraduate degree at Luther College, Decorah, Iowa, and has done graduate work in Illinois, Michigan, and North Dakota.

Index